The Art of the Exposition

Also from Westphalia Press
westphaliapress.org

The Art of the Exposition

Personal Impressions of the Architecture, Sculpture, Mural Decorations, Color Scheme & Other Aesthetic Aspects

---

by Eugen Neuhaus

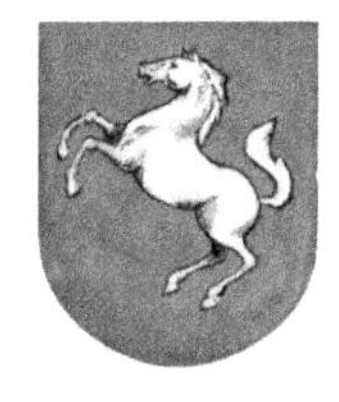

WESTPHALIA PRESS
An Imprint of Policy Studies Organization

The Art of the Exposition

Westphalia Press
An imprint of Policy Studies Organization
1527 New Hampshire Ave. NW
Washington, D.C. 20036
info@ipsonet.org

ISBN-13: 978-1-63391-681-4
ISBN-10: 1-63391-681-2

Cover design by Jeffrey Barnes:
jbarnesbook.design

Daniel Gutierrez-Sandoval, Executive Director
PSO and Westphalia Press

Updated material and comments on this edition
can be found at the Westphalia Press website:
www.westphaliapress.org

THE ART *of* THE EXPOSITION

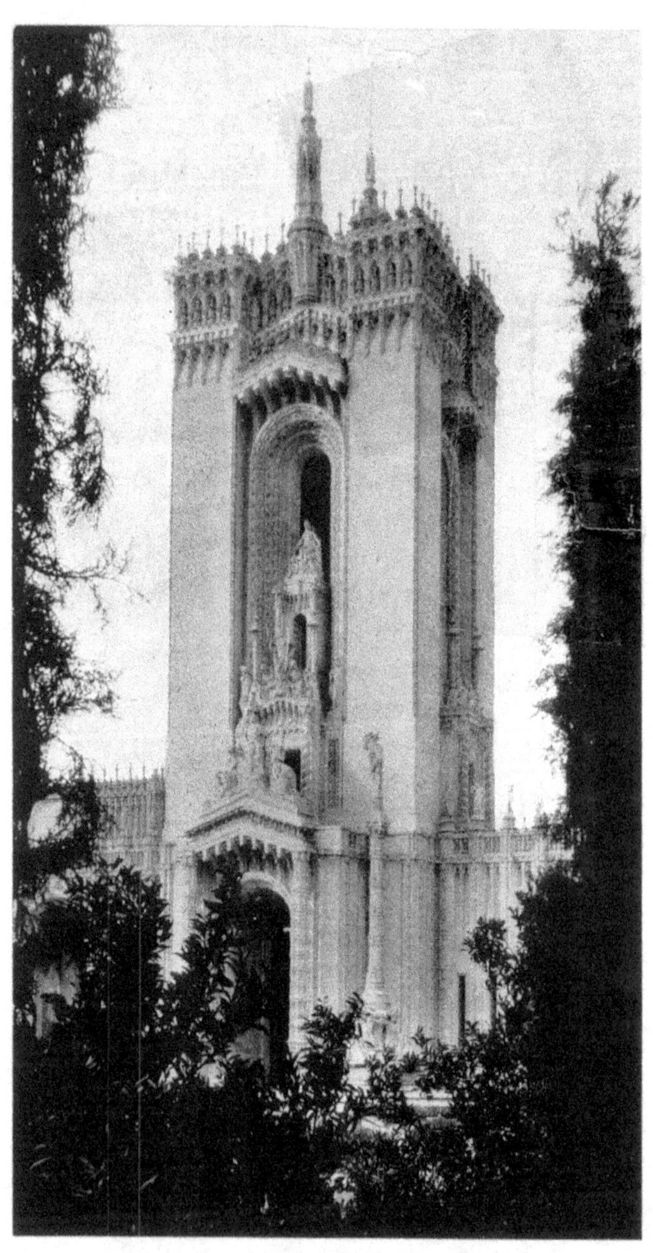

THE TOWER IN THE COURT OF ABUNDANCE
LOUIS CHRISTIAN MULLGARDT, ARCHITECT

THE ART *of* THE EXPOSITION

PERSONAL IMPRESSIONS OF THE ARCHITECTURE, SCULPTURE, MURAL DECORATIONS, COLOR SCHEME & OTHER AESTHETIC ASPECTS OF THE PANAMA-PACIFIC INTERNATIONAL EXPOSITION

By

EUGEN NEUHAUS

UNIVERSITY OF CALIFORNIA

CHAIRMAN OF THE WESTERN ADVISORY COMMITTEE AND MEMBER OF THE SAN FRANCISCO JURY IN THE DEPARTMENT OF FINE ARTS OF THE EXPOSITION

PAUL ELDER AND COMPANY
PUBLISHERS · SAN FRANCISCO

SECOND EDITION, REVISED

Publisher's Announcement

The following pages have grown out of many talks given during the year by Mr. Neuhaus to his students at the University of California. Presented to the public in the form of a series of evening lectures at the University, and repeated before many other organizations throughout California, his interpretation of the Art of the Exposition roused a demand for its repetition so widespread as only to be met by the aid of the printing press.

San Francisco, California

May 1, 1915

CONTENTS

PAGE

THE ARCHITECTURE 3
The architectural scheme, the setting and the style of the architecture.

THE SCULPTURE 26
Its relation to the architecture, its artistic meaning and its symbolism.

THE COLOR SCHEME AND THE LANDSCAPE GARDENING 48
The color elements as furnished by the artist and by nature; the horticultural effects.

THE MURAL DECORATIONS 56
The intellectual emphasis of the color scheme, and the significance of the mural decorations.

THE ILLUMINATION — CONCLUSION . 69
The Exposition at night.

APPENDIX 77
Guide to Sculpture. The Mural decorations. Biographical notes.

LIST OF ILLUSTRATIONS

FACING PAGE

The Tower in the Court of Abundance. *Louis Christian Mullgardt, Architect.* (*Frontispiece*)

Under the Arch of the Tower of Jewels. *McKim, Mead and White, Architects* 4

View Through the Great Arches of the Court of the Universe. *McKim, Mead and White, Architects* 6

Niche Detail from the Court of the Four Seasons. *Henry Bacon, Architect* 8

The Court of the Four Seasons. *Henry Bacon, Architect* . . . 10

Northern Doorway in the Court of Palms. *George Kelham, Architect* 12

Entrance into the Palace of Education. *Bliss and Faville, Architects* 14

Detail from the Court of Abundance. *Louis Christian Mullgardt, Architect* 16

The Palace of Fine Arts. *Bernard R. Maybeck, Architect* . . . 18

Colonnade, Palace of Fine Arts. *Bernard R. Maybeck, Architect.* Portal of Vigor in the Palace of Food Products (in the distance). *Bliss and Faville, Architects* 20

Colonnade, Palace of Fine Arts. *Bernard R. Maybeck, Architect* . 22

The Setting Sun. *Adolph A. Weinman, Sculptor* 28

The Nations of the West. *A. Stirling Calder, Frederick G. R. Roth, Leo Lentelli, Sculptors* 30

The Mermaid. *Arthur Putnam, Sculptor* 32

The Adventurous Bowman Supported by Frieze of Toilers—Details from the Column of Progress. *Hermon A. MacNeil, Sculptor* 34

The End of the Trail. *James Earle Fraser, Sculptor* 36

Autumn, in the Court of the Four Seasons. *Furio Piccirilli, Sculptor* 38

The Pacific—Detail from the Fountain of Energy. *A. Stirling Calder, Sculptor* 40

The Alaskan—Detail from Nations of the West. *Frederick G. R. Roth, Sculptor* 42

The Feast of Sacrifice. *Albert Jaegers, Sculptor* 44

Youth—From the Fountain of Youth. *Edith Woodman Burroughs, Sculptor* 46

Truth—Detail from the Fountain of the Setting Sun. *Adolph A. Weinman, Sculptor* 48

The Star. *A. Stirling Calder, Sculptor* 50

The Triton — Detail of the Fountain of the Rising and the Setting Sun. *Adolph A. Weinman, Sculptor* 52

Finial Figure in the Court of Abundance. *Leo Lentelli, Sculptor* . 54

Atlantic and Pacific and the Gateway of all Nations. *William de Leftwich Dodge, Painter* 56

THE ILLUSTRATIONS

FACING PAGE

Commerce, Inspiration, Truth and Religion. *Edward Simmons, Painter* 58

The Victorious Spirit. *Arthur F. Matthews, Painter* 60

The Westward March of Civilization. *Frank V. Du Mond, Painter* 62

The Pursuit of Pleasure. *Charles Halloway, Painter* 64

Primitive Fire. *Frank Brangwyn, Painter* 66

Night Effect—Colonnade of the Palace of Fine Arts. *Bernard R. Maybeck, Architect* 68

Official Poster. *Perham W. Nahl* 92

Ground Plan of the Exposition 94

THE ART *of* THE EXPOSITION

THE ARCHITECTURE

It is generally conceded that the essential lesson of the Exposition is the lesson of art. However strongly the industrial element may have asserted itself in the many interesting exhibits, no matter how extensive the appeal of the applied sciences may be, the final and lasting effect will be found in the great and enduring lesson of beauty which the Exposition so unforgetably teaches.

The visitor is at once stirred by the many manifestations of art, presented so harmoniously by the architect, the sculptor, the landscape architect, and the painter-decorator, and his attention is kept throughout by artistic appeals at every turn. It must be said in the very start that few will realize what is the simple truth—that artistically this is probably the most successful exposition ever created. It may indeed prove the last. Large international expositions are becoming a thing of the past on account of the tremendous cost for relatively temporary purposes.

There is still much of the popular conception abroad that the West has only very recently emerged from a state of semi-civilization inimical to the finer things of life, and to art in particular. But we may rest assured that the fortunate outsider who allows himself the luxury of travel will proclaim that the gospel of beauty has been preached most eloquently through the Panama-Pacific International Exposition.

The critic who prefers to condemn things will find small opportunity here, no matter how seriously he may take himself.

The first sight of that great mosaic, from the Fillmore-street hill, at once creates a nerve-soothing impression most uncommon in international expositions, and for that matter, in any architectural aggregate. One is at once struck with the fitness of the location and of the scheme of architecture. Personally, I am greatly impressed with the architectural scheme and the consistency of its application to the whole. I fear that the two men, Mr. Willis Polk and Mr. Edward Bennett, who laid the foundation for the plan, will never receive as much credit as is really due them. I hope this appreciation may serve that purpose in some small way.

It was a typically big western idea, an idea that as a rule never gets any farther than being thought of, or possibly seeing daylight as an "esquisse"—but seldom any farther than that. The Burnham plan for San Francisco was such an unrealized dream, but here the dream has achieved concrete form. The buildings as a group have all the big essential qualities that art possesses only in its noblest expression. Symmetry, balance, and harmony work together for a wonderful expression of unity, of oneness, that buildings devoted to profane purposes seldom show.

I do not know how many people who visit the Exposition are so constituted as to derive

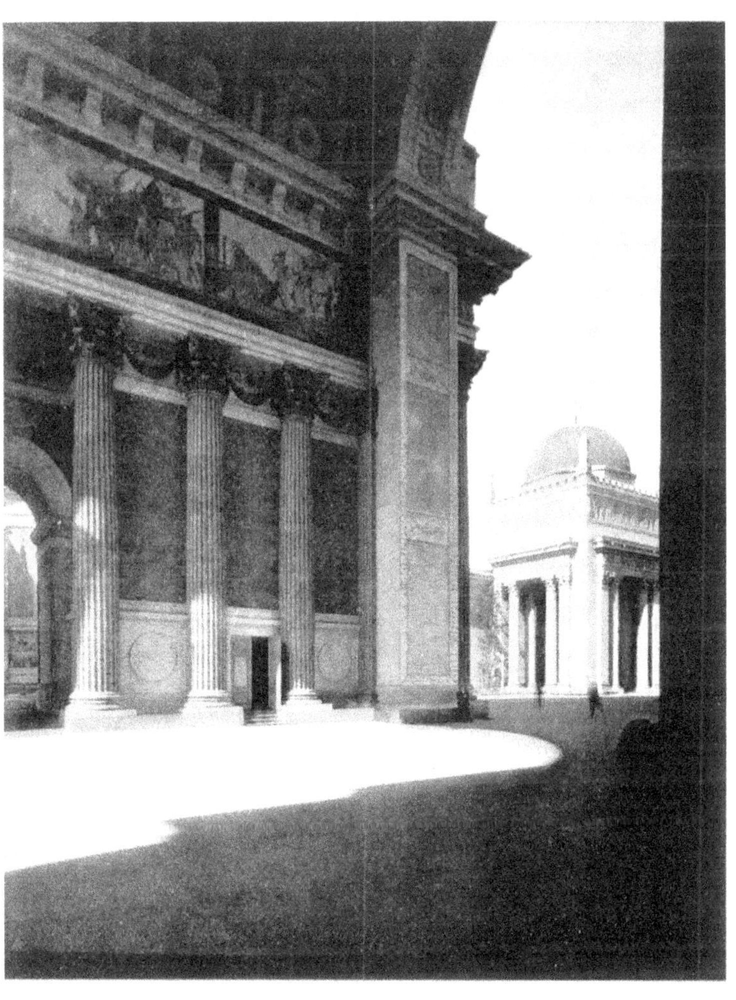

UNDER THE ARCH OF THE TOWER OF JEWELS
MC KIM, MEAD AND WHITE, ARCHITECTS

an aesthetic thrill from artistic balance, but I imagine that any person, no matter how inexperienced in matters of art, will rejoice at the fine feeling of orderly arrangement of major forms which runs through the entire grouping. It is simplicity itself, and it serves an excellent practical purpose, enabling one to visit the Exposition without being left a nervous wreck at the end.

The main entrance leads one into the physical center of the Exposition. From there, on the first visit, one realizes the existence of an equally large area on either side, covered with objects of interest.

The main exposition, composed of a compactly arranged group of large buildings of approximately equal size, is symmetrically placed on either side of the main central court, the Court of the Universe. This sends out its avenues into two equally proportioned side courts—the Court of the Four Seasons on the west and the Court of Abundance on the east. While the main court rests right in the center of the eight buildings, the side courts fit snugly into the center of the four buildings on either side. This arrangement of large masses, comprising the bulk of the Exposition, creates a grateful feeling of repose and of order, without being in the least uninteresting, for while there is perfect symmetry, on the one hand, in the larger masses, there is plenty and ever changing variety in the minor architectural forms and embellishments. The same balance, the same interesting distribution of architectural masses, continues on either side of the main building. In Machinery

Hall, on the one hand, and the Fine Arts Palace on the western side, perfect balance is again maintained. That is, however, not the end of it all. Loosening up in a very subtle way, we find cleverly arranged the buildings of the various States of the Union and of Foreign Nations on the western side of the Fine Arts Palace, while at the other extremity of the main group, screened by Machinery Hall, is the amusement section, officially labelled "The Zone."

I do not suspect that the Zone is intended to give any artistic thrills. If so, I would propose to call it "The Limit," and so I drop it as a subject for further artistic reference. It is invaluable, however, as an object lesson in showing the fatal results of the utter disregard of all those fundamental laws of balance, harmony, and unity so uniformly and persistently applied through the seriously designed main body of the Exposition. There is no harmony whatever in the Zone anywhere, either in the form, style, or color, unless it be the harmony of ugliness which is carried through this riotous mêlée of flimsiness and sham. I cannot help but feel that this hodge-podge will convince the most doubting Thomas who might believe in the mob rule of hundreds of conflicting tastes. The Zone is not an improvement on similar things in former Expositions. Save for certain minor exceptions at the entrance, it will serve as a wonderfully effective illustration of the taste of the great masses of the people, and as a fine business investment.

So far, we have moved only along the east and west axis of the Exposition. The north and

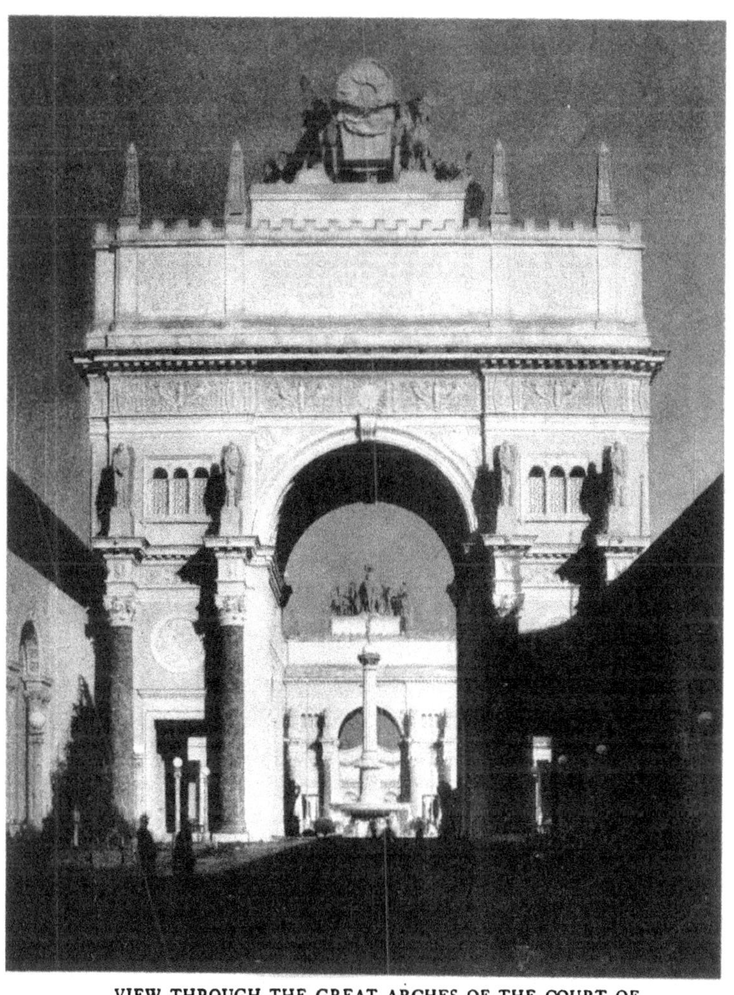

VIEW THROUGH THE GREAT ARCHES OF THE COURT OF THE UNIVERSE
MC KIM, MEAD AND WHITE, ARCHITECTS

south development is not without its charm. The terraced city of San Francisco, on the south, without a doubt looks best on a densely foggy day. With its fussy, incongruous buildings—I hesitate to call them architecture—it serves hardly as a background for anything, let alone a group of monumental buildings. The opposite side, where nature reigns, atones for multitudes of sins that man committed on the city's hills. But how great an opportunity there was lost! There are, however, some indications at the western end of Broadway that give fine promise for the future.

The bay and its background of rising hills and blue mountain sides provide the wonderful setting that so charmingly holds the Exposition. The general arrangement of the Exposition pays its respects to the bay at every possible angle. The vistas from the three courts towards the bay are the pièces de résistance of the whole thing. It was a fine idea, not alone from an economic point of view, to eliminate the two arches which appeared in the original plan at the end of the avenues running north from the Court of the Four Seasons and the Court of Abundance. There is hardly anything more inspiring than to stand in any of the three courts and to look north through those well proportioned colonnades over the blue bay towards the purple foothills of Marin County, crowned by the graceful slopes of Mount Tamalpais on one side and the many islands of the bay on the other. It is surprising into how many enchanting vistas the whole arrangement resolves itself. For the city-planner the Exposition contains a wonderful lesson. What fine cities we might have if some artistic control could be exercised over the buildings which are to stand opposite the junction of one street with another, not only at right angles, but also at lesser degrees—for instance, in all cases of streets running into Market street from the northwest.

To point out some particularly fine vistas, among many, we should mention that from the Orchestral Niche in the Court of the Four Seasons, looking toward the bay, or from the same court toward the Fine Arts Palace—and many more. The natural background seems to have been considered always, even in the arrangements of the smallest apertures. One should not overlook the two open courts which run off the main avenue, like charming coves in an island, into the main group of buildings, connecting at their ends with the Court of the Four Seasons at the west and the Court of Abundance toward the east. These two, the Court of Palms and the Court of Flowers, have not so much the charm of seclusion of the more centrally located courts, but their architecture makes them of great interest.

As to the style of the architecture of the main group of eight buildings, it has been called classic. If one means by that something excellent, something in good taste, we must admit that it is classic indeed. However, on closer examination it becomes very evident that the individuality of many men has found expression in the architectural structural forms, as well as in the minor and decorative forms.

The main Tower of Jewels, by Carrère and Hastings, marking the center of the whole

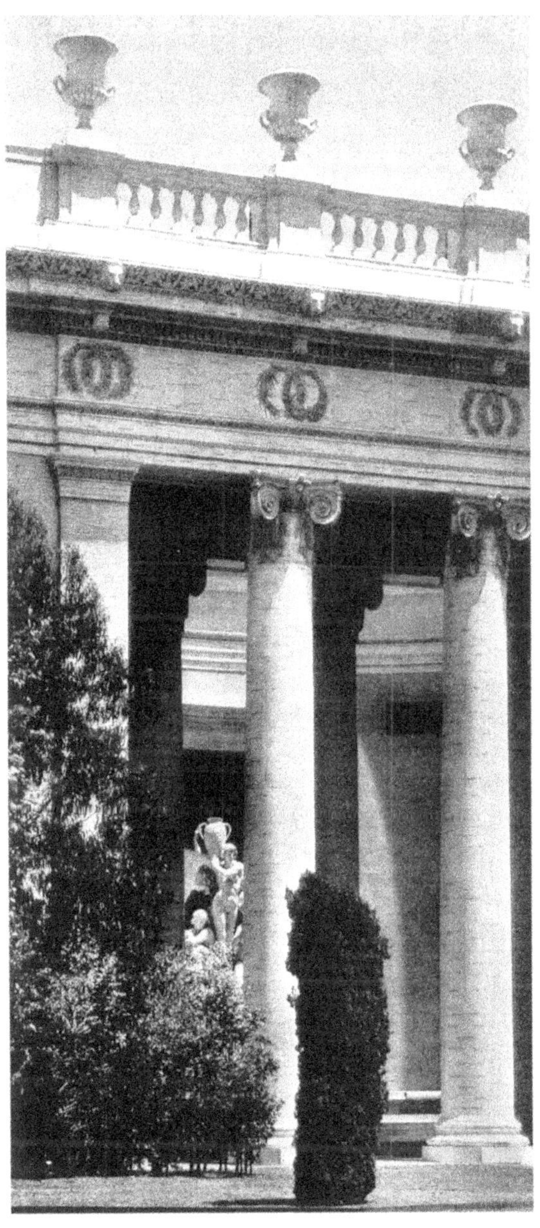

NICHE DETAIL FROM THE COURT OF THE FOUR SEASONS
HENRY BACON, ARCHITECT

scheme, has a distinct character of its own. There is no doubt that it is effective, but while its chief merit lies in its colossal proportions and its relative position, I feel that it lacks that oneness of conception that characterizes almost every other architectural unit in the Exposition. One feels too much the stacking up of story after story, that effort to fill the requirements of a given great height, very much as a boy sets up blocks of diminishing size, one on top of the other, until he can go no further because there are no smaller blocks. The whole effect of the tower is too static. Of its architectural motives, almost too many seem devoid of much interest, and like the column motive, repeated too often. The very effective and decorative employment of "jewels" tends to loosen up and enliven the structure very much. On a sunny day the effect is dazzling and joyous. The tower has a feeling of dignity and grandeur, commensurate with its scale and setting. However, its great height is not apparent, owing largely to its breadth of base. The Sather Campanile in Berkeley looks higher, though it is actually one hundred and thirty-three feet lower. The side towers at the entrances of the Court of Palms and the Court of Flowers, while not so imaginative as the main tower, are far more sky-reaching. As towers go, John Galen Howard's tower at the Buffalo Exposition in 1901 stands unsurpassed in every way as an Exposition tower.

The main Court of Honor, or Court of the Universe, as it is also called, designed by McKim, Mead and White, impresses by its tremendous dimensions, which operate somewhat against its proper enjoyment. I believe that the court is too large—so many things are lost in it, and it does not convey the quality of shelter that the two lesser courts possess in such marked degree. The Court of the Universe will never be the resting place of the masses of the people, in spite of the recently added attraction of the band stand, a mixture of Roman and Arabic architecture out of keeping with the surroundings. The conventional architectural motives of this great court do not help very much in tempting one to stay, and if it were not for the great arches on the east and west and the very fine view toward the Column of Progress, I would feel tempted to classify it as a piece of architectural design of the stereotyped variety. It has all the great qualities and faults of the court in front of St. Peter's in Rome. There is too little play of landscape gardening in and near the Court of the Universe, a condition which will remedy itself with the breaking into bloom of the great masses of rhododendron which have been installed in the sunken garden in the center.

Like all careful interpretations in the classic architectural traditions, the Court of the Universe has a great feeling of dignity and grandeur, which gives the visitor a feeling of the big scale of the rest of the architecture. The court lacks, however, the individual note of the two side courts.

Toward the west, passing through a very characteristic avenue, in the style of the happiest phases of the Italian Renaissance to be found in Florence, one enters the Court of the Four

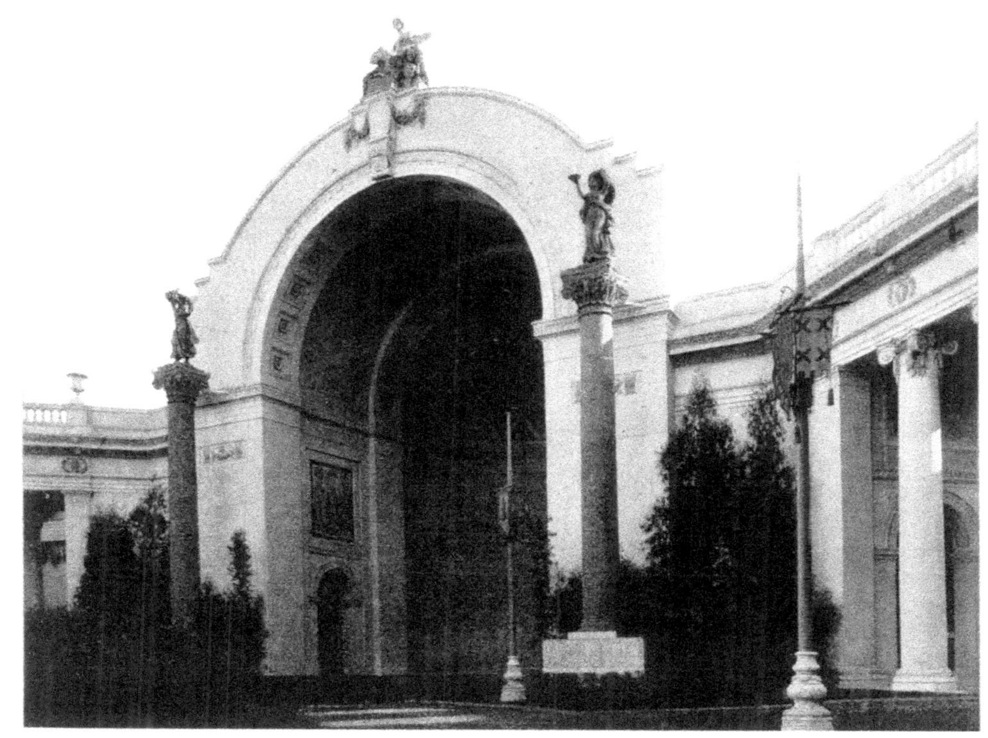

THE COURT
OF THE FOUR
SEASONS
HENRY BACON,
ARCHITECT

Seasons, by Henry Bacon of New York. The chief quality of this court is that of intimacy. While by no means so original as the Court of Abundance, it has a charm all of its own, in spite of its conventional architectural characteristics, which are really not different from those of the main Court of Honor. However, a very happy combination of gardening effects and architecture, together with the interesting wall-fountains, screened by stately rows of columns, make for a picture of great loveliness. Of all the courts, it has the most inviting feeling of seclusion. The plain body of water in the center, without statuary of any kind, is most effective as a mirror reflecting the play of lights and shadows, which are so important an asset in this enchanting retreat. During the Exposition it will serve as a recreation center for many people who will linger in the seclusion of the groups of shrubbery and watch the shadows of the afternoon sun creep slowly up the surrounding walls.

As an Exposition feature, the Court of the Four Seasons is a decided innovation. At St. Louis, for instance, in 1904, everything seemed to have been done to excite, to overstimulate, to develop a craving for something new, to make one look for the next thing. Here, in the Court of the Four Seasons, one wants to stay. Most emphatically one wants to rest for awhile and give one's self over entirely to that feeling of liberation that one experiences in a church, in the forest, or out on the ocean. I could stay in this court forever. To wander into this Court of the Four Seasons from any one of the many approaches is equally satisfactory, and it will prove a very popular and successful Exposition innovation.

Speaking of the courts, one is bound to yield to the individual note of Louis Mullgardt's Court of Abundance, on the east of the Court of the Universe. Of all the courts it has, without a doubt, the strongest individual note. It seems on first acquaintance to be reminiscent of the Gothic, of which it has, no doubt, the quality of lightness, the laciness, and the play of many fine apertures and openings. It has, however, neither the Gothic arch nor the buttresses of that period, and so far as its ground plan goes, it is thoroughly original. It looks as if carved out of a solid block of stone. This monolithic quality is particularly well brought out in the tower on the north. While not quite so intimate as the Court of the Four Seasons, it conveys a feeling of shelter and seclusion very well by showing an uninterrupted wall motive on all sides. The sculpture symbolism of this court is particularly fine. We shall return to it in a consideration of sculpture.

The two minor courts by George Kelham are particularly fortunate in their open location toward the south. Their sheltered and warm atmosphere is quite in keeping with the suggestion of Spanish Renaissance which has been employed in the constructive and in the many decorative motives. The western court, or Court of Palms, is made particularly attractive by a sunken garden effect and pool. The effect of the Court of Flowers is similar in every way to its mate on the east.

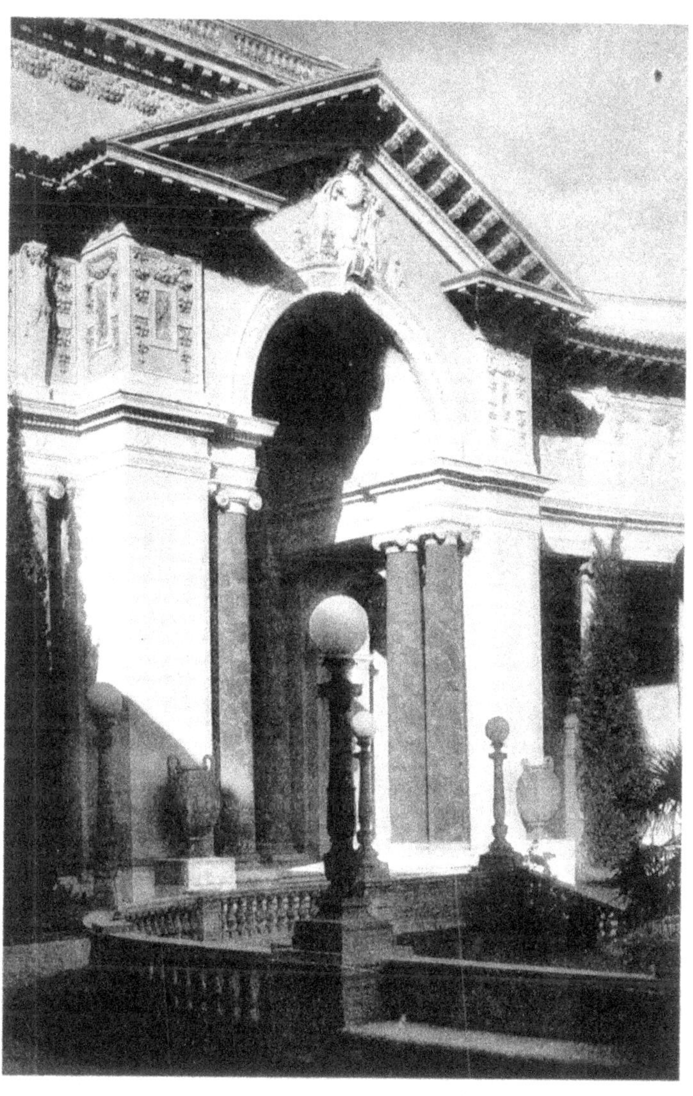

NORTHERN DOORWAY IN THE COURT OF PALMS
GEORGE W. KELHAM, ARCHITECT

A consideration of these two courts, with their towers, leads easily into a study of the outer façade, which, so to speak, ties all of the eight Palaces together into a compact, snug arrangement, so typical of the Exposition.

Bliss and Faville of San Francisco are responsible for the very skillful use of simple, plain surfaces, accentuated and relieved here and there by ornate doorways, wall-fountains, niches, and half-domes. On the south, along the Avenue of Palms, are found some very fine adaptations of old Spanish doorways, which deserve to be preserved. It is regrettable that we have no large museum on the coast where these fine doorways in the outer walls of the Palace of Varied Industries could be preserved permanently. The travertine marble has nowhere been used more effectively than in just such details. The entrance of the Palace of Education at the western end of the south façade is also of great beauty of design.

On the western end two huge niches or half-domes command attention by their noble beauty and fine setting amidst great clumps of eucalyptus. On the north, no special effort has been made. There is, however, a decorative emphasis of the doorways along the entire front. On the east, facing the Palace of Machinery, some very fine doorways, very much like some of the minor ones on the south, furnish the decoration. It was no small task to bridge the many diversified architectural motives which penetrate into the outer wall from within, in the shape of many avenues and courts, and one can appreciate the difficulties of the designer who met so well these conflicting requirements.

Of the detached palaces outside of the eight forming the rectangular block nucleus, the Palace of Machinery attracts by its enormous size. I am not interested in how many kegs of nails and iron bolts and washers went into its anatomy. They add nothing to the artistic enjoyment of this very massive building. One point, however, in connection with the liberal use of the raw material is of artistic significance, and that is that the internal structural aspects of this great palace, as well as of the others, are not without charm and interest. It is only in recent years, and particularly in America, that the engineer has dared to invade the realm of the artist by attempting to make the constructive, anatomical material, like uprights, bracings, trusses, and beams, assume artistic responsibilities. It has been for many years the custom to expect the engineer to do his share in obscurity with the idea that it ultimately will be covered up by the work of the architect. The extraordinary development of engineering in this country, to meet new and original problems, sometimes of colossal proportions, particularly in the field of concrete design, has resulted in some conditions heretofore entirely unknown. I feel with much satisfaction that the unobscured appearance of the wood construction in the Palace of Machinery is very pleasing, owing to its sound constructive elements, as well as to a very fine regard for pattern-making in the placing of the bolts and braces. Here we discover the engineer in the role of the artist, which he seems to enjoy, and which offers endless new opportunities, particularly in the field

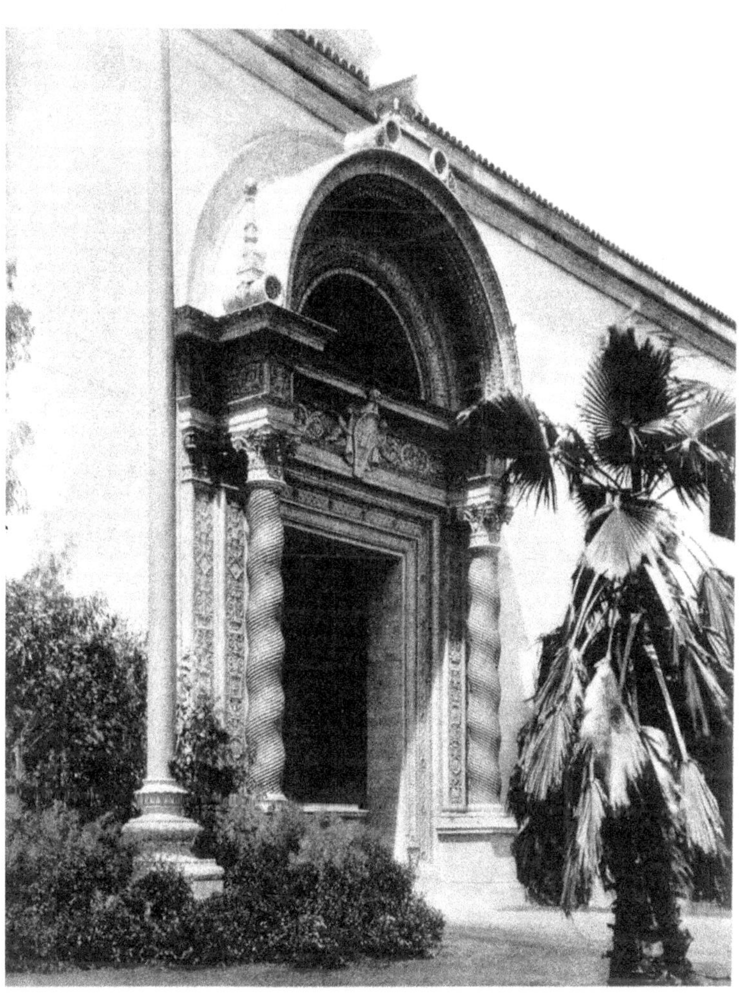

ENTRANCE INTO THE PALACE OF EDUCATION
BLISS AND FAVILLE, ARCHITECTS

of concrete construction, as well as in wood. The great size of the Machinery Palace is much more enjoyable from within, on account of the constructive patterns left in the raw, than from without, where there is not enough animation in the many plain surfaces of the outer walls. I do not know that it is customary to put the engineer's name, together with that of the architect, on a building; the time is approaching very rapidly when we shall be in duty bound to do so.

Aside from the structural charm of the inside, the outer façade of Machinery Hall is not entirely devoid of architectural interest. Its general forms are apparently those of an early Christian church, although its decorative motives are all indicative of the profane purposes for which it is used.

Festival Hall, by Farquhar, of Los Angeles, at the east end of the south gardens, does not look particularly festive, and it is not original enough to shine by itself, like its very happy mate at the south end, the Horticultural Palace. There is nothing like this Horticultural Palace anywhere on the grounds in its gorgeous richness of decorative adornment. It has no relation to any other building on the site. It is very happy, with its many joyous garlands, flower-baskets, and suggestions of horticultural forms—all very well done—so very much better done than so many of the cheap period imitations so common to our residence districts. It is so decidedly joyous in character that people looking for Festival Hall wander over to the Horticultural Palace, attracted by the very joyousness of its scheme.

Good rococo ornamentation is rare abroad and even rarer in this country, which is essentially opposed in its tendencies and in its civilization to those luxurious days of the French kings who created the conditions under which this very delightful style could flourish.

The Horticultural Palace is a great success as an interpretation of a style which rarely finds a sympathetic expression in this country. I do not feel at all that it ought, but in a case of this kind where a temporary purpose existed, it was happily chosen.

Of all isolated units, none causes greater admiration than the Fine Arts Palace. It presents the astounding spectacle of a building which violates the architectural conventions on more than one occasion, and in spite of it, or possibly for that very reason, it has a note of originality that is most conspicuous. Everybody admits that it is most beautiful, and very few seem to know just how this was accomplished. Many of the "small fry" of the architectural profession enjoy themselves in picking out its faults, which are really, as suggested above, the reason for its supreme beauty. Save for Mullgardt's court, it is the only building that seems to be based on the realization of a dream of a true artistic conception. With many other of the buildings one feels the process of their creation in the time-honored, pedantic way. They are paper-designed by the mechanical application of the "T" square and the triangle. They do not show the advantage of having been experienced as a vision.

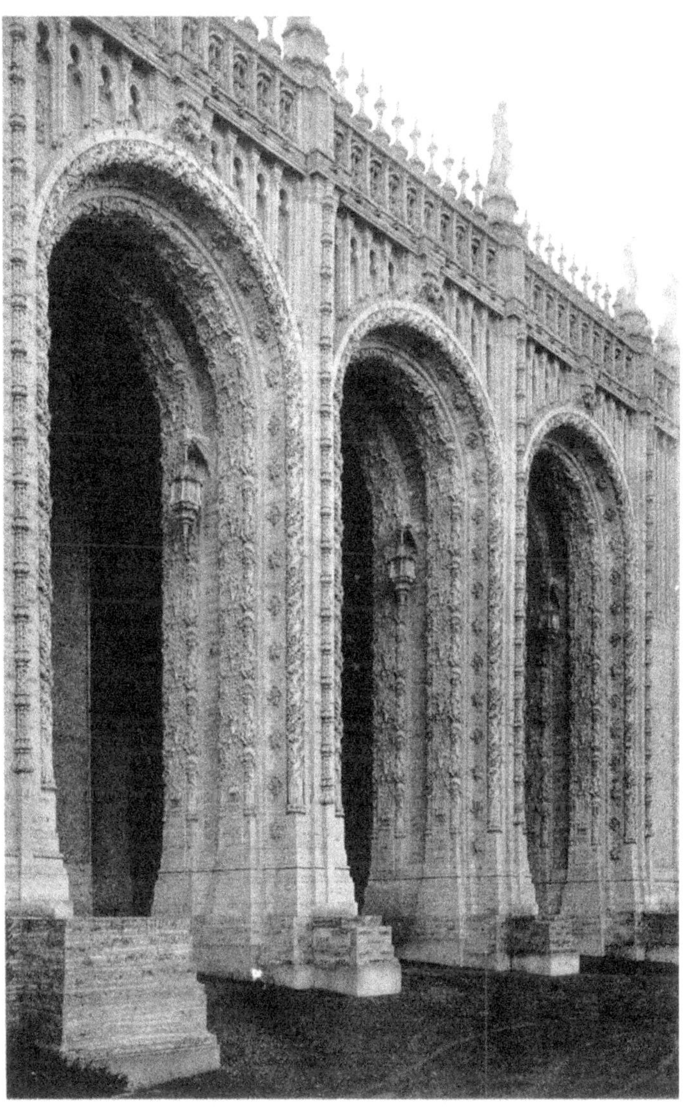

DETAIL FROM THE COURT OF ABUNDANCE
LOUIS CHRISTIAN MULLGARDT, ARCHITECT

With Bernard Maybeck's Palace of Fine Arts, one has the feeling that this great temple is a realized dream; that it was imagined irrespective of time, cost, or demand. Like all of Maybeck's buildings, it is thoroughly original. Of course the setting contributes much to the picturesque effect, but aside from that, the colonnades and the octagonal dome in the center of the semi-circular embracing form of the main building present many interesting features There is a very fine development of vistas, which are so provided as to present different parts of the building in many ever-changing aspects. On entering the outer colonnade one forgets the proximity of everyday things; one is immediately in an atmosphere of religious devotion, which finds its noblest expression in that delicate shrine of worship, by Ralph Stackpole, beneath the dome. This spiritual quality puts the visitor into the proper frame of mind for the enjoyment of the other offerings of art within the building. Mr. Maybeck has demonstrated once again that his talent is equal to any task in the field of architectural art. I wish we had more of his rare kind and more people to do justice to his genius.

Not far from the Palace of Fine Arts, on the shores of the bay, the monumental tower of the California building fits well into the scheme of things. Seen from a distance, from numerous points across the lagoon, it offers a great many effective compositions in connection with some very decorative groups of old acacia trees, the legacy of an old amusement park of the bygone days of San Francisco—the old Harbor View

Gardens. In the shade of these old trees a fine old formal garden of exquisite charm, screened from the eyes of the intruder by an old clipped Monterey cypress hedge, really constitutes the unique note of this typically Mission building. The architect, Mr. Burditt, deserves great credit for an unusually respectful treatment of a very fine architectural asset. This very enchanting old flower garden, with its sundial and cozy nooks, has an intimate feeling throughout, and it furnishes the delightful suggestive note of old age, of historical interest, without which it would never have been convincing.

Aside from the outdoor features, the building, exclusive of the county annex, discloses a very fine talent in a very happy combination of classic tradition and modern tendencies. The building is altogether very successful, in a style which is so much made use of but which is really devoid of any distinct artistic merit. Most of the examples of the so-called "Mission style" in California are very uninteresting in their decorative motives, however big their ground plans may be in their liberal use of space.

The Oregon building is just across the way from the California building, and as an object of artistic analysis it is a most interesting single unit. Personally, I am not enthusiastic over it. It was most decidedly a very illogical idea to select a building to represent Oregon from a country which has nothing whatever in common with this northern state. One could hardly discover a more arid country, devoid of vegetation, particularly of trees, than Greece; and to compare it with the apparently inex-

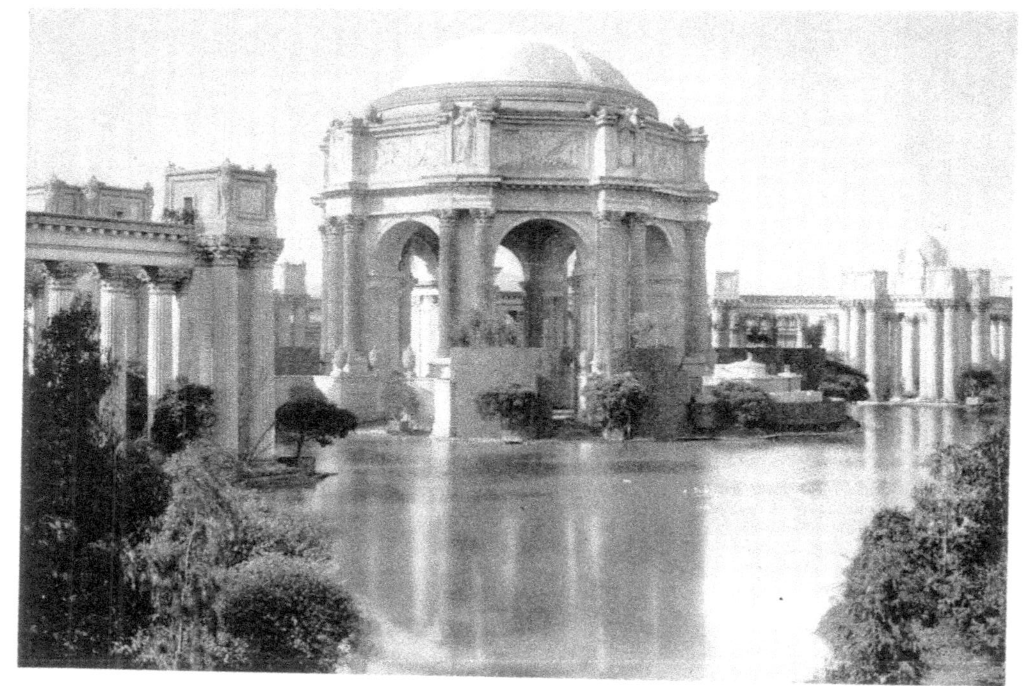

THE PALACE OF FINE ARTS
BERNARD R. MAYBECK, ARCHITECT

haustible wealth of virgin forests of Oregon makes the contrast almost grotesque. Besides, a building like the Parthenon, designed to grace and terminate the top of a hill, is surely not adapted for a flat piece of ground like the Exposition field. And in the choice of material used in its construction it shows a lack of appreciation for the fitness of things generally. The Parthenon was designed to be made in stone, as much for the construction as for the light color effect of the marble. Only the light color play of its exterior would do against a placid blue sky to relieve the otherwise exceedingly simple rigidity of its massive forms of construction. To make an imitation of this great building in uncouth, somber, almost black pine logs of dubious proportions is hardly an artistically inspired accomplishment.

There must always be a certain regard for the use of the right material in the right place. A wooden bridge will disclose its material even to the uninitiated at a very great distance, because everybody knows that certain things can be done only in wood. A stone, concrete, iron, or cable bridge, for example, will each always look its part, out of sheer material and structural necessity. A log house would have been far better and more successful than this pseudo Parthenon. It is in the same class with the statues of Liberty made from walnuts that are the great attractions in our autumnal agricultural shows. The State of Oregon, however, is well represented by a fine immense flagpole, which could hardly have been cut anywhere else than on the Pacific Coast.

Of other state buildings in this neighborhood, a number are impressive by their cost, like the New York building; others, again, by historical suggestions of great charm. There are several which reflect in a very interesting way the Colonial days of early American history; and buildings like those of New Jersey and Virginia, in spite of their unpretentiousness, are very successful. Nobody would take them for anything else but what they represent.

The Pennsylvania building shows a very fine combination of the classic and of the modern. It was originally designed to hold the Liberty Bell. In order to avoid the necessity of building a fireproof building, the open hall was adopted, with its inviting spaciousness, and two lower enclosing wings at the side. The arrangement of the Pennsylvania building is formal, owing to its symmetry, but not at all heavy. Its decorative detail is full of interest, and to discover Hornbostel of New York, the designer of the Oakland City Hall, as the author of this building, is a pleasant surprise.

Of most of the other state buildings, really nothing original could be claimed. They are, on the whole, dignified in their classic motives, and in most cases, in better taste than the many foreign buildings.

Among these, the buildings representing Sweden, Denmark, Norway, Italy, and Bolivia, must claim particular attention. It must seem strange that the three northern countries named first should excel in originality of architecture, as well as in the allied arts.

The Swedish building, designed by Ferdinand Boberg, presents admirably his great

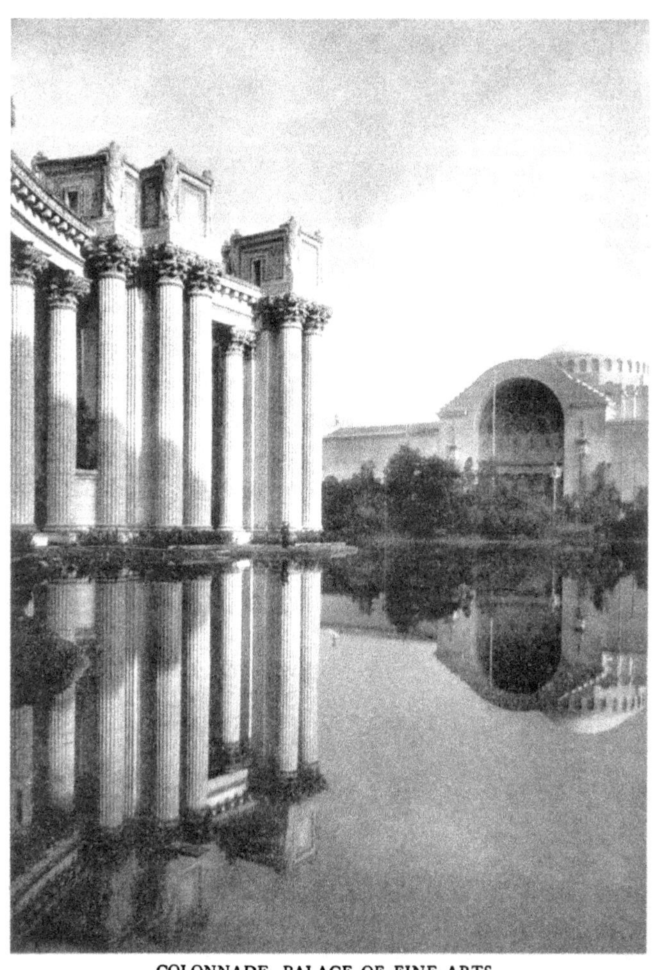

COLONNADE, PALACE OF FINE ARTS
BERNARD R. MAYBECK, ARCHITECT
PORTAL OF VIGOR IN THE PALACE OF FOOD PRODUCTS
IN THE DISTANCE
BLISS AND FAVILLE, ARCHITECTS

talent. The name "Boberg" means nothing to most people out here, but anybody at all familiar with the development of modern architecture abroad will always think of Boberg as the greatest living master of Swedish architecture. His very talented wife, Anna Boberg, is equally well represented in another department, that of the Fine Arts.

The plan of the Swedish building is unsymmetrical, but well balanced, nevertheless. The typical northern wood tower, at one side, has a very fine outline, and like the roof, has a very fine decorative shingle covering, interesting in pattern as well as in color. I am very much tempted to speak of the treasures found inside of this building, but we must go on to Denmark's building.

This building, situated near the southern end of the Fine Arts Colonnade, has a far more advantageous location than the Swedish building. Situated on a narrow tongue of triangular shape, the architect has taken the fullest advantage of this original piece of ground. The building gives a very good idea of some of the very best tendencies in the modern art of Europe, without being bizarre, like some recent American attempts in the most wrongly labeled of all art expressions—the "Art Nouveau."

The Norwegian building, somewhat remotely situated, back of the French building and near the Presidio entrance, has very much in common with the Swedish building, and offers the same attractive features of wood and stone construction as the building representing its sister state. Historical traditions and everything else are so much alike in these two countries that it must not surprise one to find the two buildings have so many points of interest in common.

The north of Europe has given to the world many very excellent and genuine expressions of architecture, which, owing to their fine constructive qualities, have been absorbed wherever wood is the principal building material. The art contributions of Sweden, Norway, and Denmark will long remain in the memory of all Exposition visitors.

Holland makes considerable pretensions as to originality of style in a curiously incongruous creation at the north of the Fine Arts Palace. During the last twenty years a peculiarly inadaptable type of building has been developed in Holland by a group of younger architects. Many of these buildings are suggestive of stone rather than of brick construction, and they do not fit in very well into the architectural traditions of the Dutch—builders traditionally of the finest brick structures in the world.

The Holland building at the Exposition is not typical of that great and independent people. It looks cheap and has all the faults of the Art Nouveau, which has, unfortunately, been much discredited by just such things in our own country, where classical traditions are so firmly and so persistently entrenched.

While structurally this building is of a peculiar, affected, ultra-modern note, the general scheme of decoration inside as well as outside compels much praise. The general feeling of refinement, of serenity, that so strongly characterizes the interior is due to the able work of

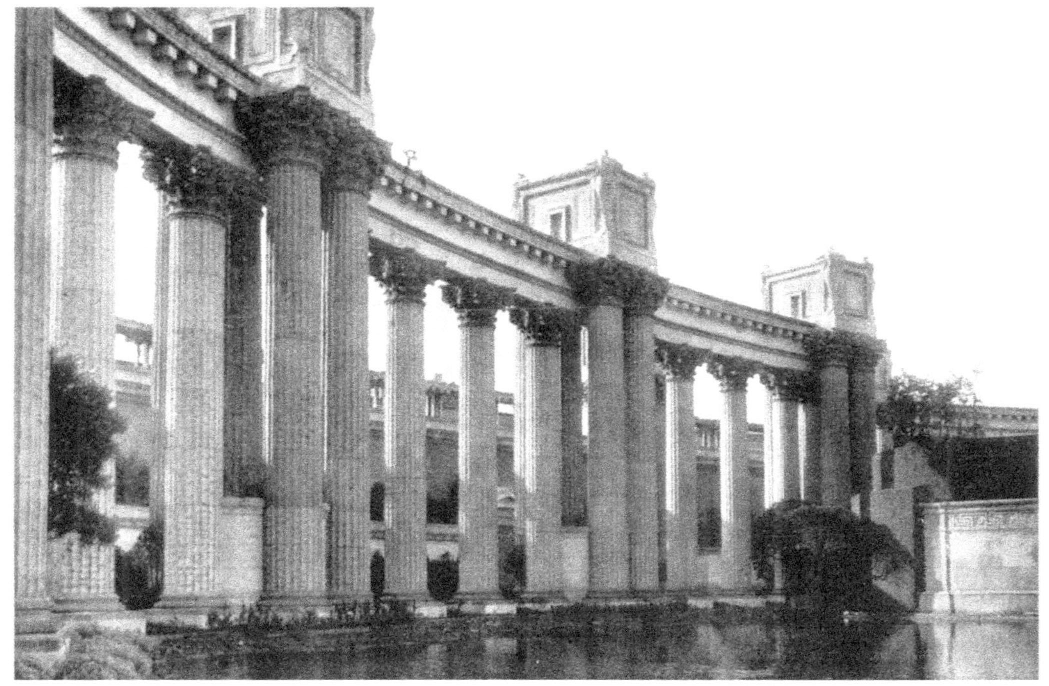

COLONNADE,
PALACE OF FINE
ARTS
BERNARD R. MAYBECK,
ARCHITECT

Hermann Rosse, a capable decorator-painter, who designed and supervised the entire color scheme.

The color scheme inside the Holland building, while daring, is most original in using an unusual combination of steel-blue and warm grey silver tones. These two relatively cold notes are enhanced in a complementary color sense by touches of orange and yellow. A constructive stencil pattern based on the two national plants of Holland, the orange tree and the tulip, add richness to the general effect. Mr. Rosse's very decorative wall painting opposite the main entrance represents the Industries of Peace. While somewhat severe, it adds dignity in motive as well as in treatment.

On the outside some fine decorative tile panels reflect one of the chief industries of the Dutch and also tell of the influence that Dutch art has long received from Holland's East Indian possessions. These tile panels are very decorative. To us, out here, they suggest artistic ceramic possibilities for architectural purposes of which we have taken little advantage. Considering the fact that we have quantities of good clay and that so much original good decorative design is lying idle, this inactivity in architectural ceramics in California is distressing. So far as I know, Batchelder, in Pasadena, still has the monopoly on architectural tiles for the entire Pacific coast.

Other European countries besides Holland are interestingly represented. The Italian building is a dignified building of pure Florentine Renaissance lines, with here and there a modern note.

This should rather be called a group of buildings, since it is a combination of some of the finest bits of Italian Renaissance architecture. The architects of this building succeeded admirably in giving a feeling of antiquity to the general treatment of the whole arrangement, which, under the blue sky of California, brings one straight back into the land of sunshine and artistic tradition. The whole arrangement of this Italian group seems somewhat bewildering at first, but on closer inspection resolves itself into a very interesting scheme which takes full advantage of the irregularly shaped site.

There is a most impressive noble dignity in the hall of the main building, where mural decorations of figural character add much to the sumptuousness of the general effect. It is remarkable how in this age of low ceilings a return to great height for rooms, as in these Italian chambers, produces a marked note of originality. The light effect created in this way, in all of these replicas of the mansions of the wealthy of the Renaissance period, is most helpful in the display of a multitude of lovely objects—furniture, jewelry, ceramics, tapestries, and yet more. The sculptural imitations of so many old pieces of statuary are not in very good taste. They bear too much the traces of the pneumatic drill, and most of them are cold and devoid of the spirit of the original. Some of the very modern marbles in the various rooms are almost pathetic in their disregard for the standards established by the forefathers of their creators.

France, unfortunately, does not rise above the commonplace, in an extensive building hastily constructed. And Portugal is shining in all the glory of wedding-cake ornamentation that the plaster of Paris artist could produce.

South America appears in a very typical building representing Bolivia. It is evident that it was not a costly building, but its dignified Spanish façade and the court effect inside are far more agreeable than the pretentious palace erected by the Argentine Republic.

The Orient, with the oldest art traditions in the world, can justly be expected to outdo the rest of the world. We find Japan again, as on previous occasions, excelling in its typical arrangement of a number of small pavilions in an irregular garden. The entire Japanese display, architectural and all, is so perfect a unit that one cannot speak of the buildings alone without thinking of the gardens. The Japanese sense of detail and love of the picturesque are disclosed at every turn. We still have with us in San Francisco, as a memento of the Midwinter Fair of 1894, the Japanese Garden in Golden Gate Park, and while this new creation at the Exposition is not so extensive, it is none the less charming.

In contrast to the Japanese wonderland near the Inside Inn, the new Republic of China seems to be very unhappily represented, not very far away. The whole Chinese ensemble seems a riot of terrible colors, devoid of all the mellow qualities of Oriental art. If China's art was retired with the Manchu dynasty, then I hope the new Republic will soon die a natural death.

THE SCULPTURE

THE sculptural decorations of the Exposition are so much a part of the architectural scheme that their consideration must no longer be delayed. The employment of sculpture has been most judicious and has never lost sight of certain architectural requirements, so frequently overlooked. While there are a great many examples of sculptural decorations at the Exposition, there does not seem to be that over-abundance of ornamentation so often confused by the public with artistic effect.

The best compliment that can be paid to the Exposition sculpture is that it is not evident at first and that one becomes aware of it only in the course of studying the architecture. I do not think that, with the exception of the Column of Progress and the groups of the Nations of the East and of the West, the Exposition has produced, through its very unusual and novel opportunities, any great work, or presented any new talent heretofore not recognized; but it will most certainly stand a critical examination and comparison with other Exposition sculpture and not suffer thereby. As a matter of fact, a number of the sculptors of our Exposition were commissioned to do similar work at St. Louis.

In one respect our Exposition must immediately claim originality—that is, in the elimination of the glaring white, with its many ugly and distracting reflected lights, insisted upon for years, in practically all the great expositions of the past. This absence of white is surely a very novel and very helpful feature, from an artistic point of view. The Travertine staff material used, the highly successful work of Mr. Paul Denneville, with its innumerable fine accidental effects, so reminiscent of the tone and the weatherbeaten qualities of really old surfaces, is an asset that the sculptors among all the collaborating artists gratefully acknowledge.

The artistic value of the Travertine lies in its beautiful expression of architecture as well as of sculpture. A plain wall becomes a matter of interest and comfort. An ornamental feature or sculpture obtains a wonderful charm and delicacy in this material which is particularly unique in sculpture. The natural Travertine is a sedimentary deposit dating back, it is claimed, to the glacial ages. That imitated here forms the bed of the River Tiber near Rome and was extensively used for ages in the early Roman and Greek era as a building stone for their temples and works of art. While a poor material in cold climates, because of its striation, it was always sought in Italy for its wonderful texture and tone. It was used in the Coliseum and in many other buildings erected during the Roman period.

It is evident that there has been a very happy and close co-operation between the architect and the sculptor—a desirable condition that, unfortunately, does not always exist. Architects will sometimes not allow the sculptor to give full expression to his ideas, will put unwarranted restrictions upon him, and the result is very one-sided.

I had the pleasure of seeing much of the sculpture grow from the sketch to the finished full-scale work, and the kindliness and the vigorous personality of Mr. Stirling Calder added much charm and interest to this experience. Mr. Calder has been the director of the department of sculpture and the inspiration of his own work penetrates that of all his fellow-artists. Among them are many specialists, such as Frederick Roth, for instance, as a modeler of animals, who shows in the very fine figure of "The Alaskan" in the Nations of the West that he is not afraid nor unable to model human figures. Practically all of the animals in the grounds show the hand of Roth.

Like Roth, Leo Lentelli did a good share of the task. His work is characterized by much animation and spirit, but well balanced wherever necessary, by a feeling of wise restraint. I remember with much horror some of the sculptural atrocities of former expositions that seemed to jump off pedestals they were intended to inhabit for a much longer period than they were apparently willing. Repose and restraint, as a rule, are lacking in much of our older American sculpture, as some of our Market-street statuary testifies. It seems that our unsettled conditions find an echo in our art. It is much to be hoped that a certain craving for temporary excitement will be replaced by a wholesome appreciation of those more enduring qualities of repose and balance.

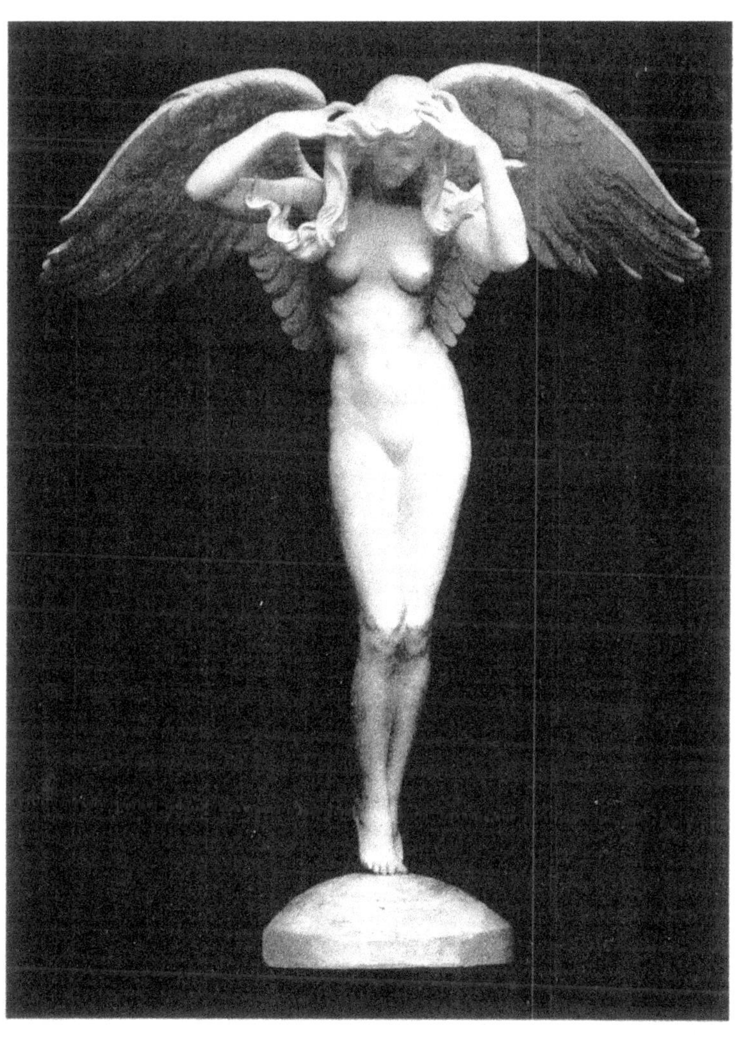

THE SETTING SUN
ADOLPH A. WEINMAN, SCULPTOR

Calder's work, no matter how animated, no matter how full of action, is always reposeful. His "Fountain of Energy" gives a good idea of what I mean. It is the first piece of detached sculpture that greets the Exposition visitor. Its position at the main gate, in the South Gardens, in front of the Tower of Jewels, is the most prominent place the Exposition offers. It is worthy of its maker's talent. Its main quality is a very fine, stimulating expression of joyousness that puts the visitor at once in a festive mood. The Fountain of Energy is a symbol of the vigor and daring of our mighty nation, which carried to a successful ending a gigantic task abandoned by another great republic. The whole composition is enjoyable for its many fine pieces of detail. Beginning at the base, one observes the huge bulks of fanciful sea-beasts, carrying on their backs figures representing the four principal oceans of the world: the North and South Arctic, the Atlantic, and the Pacific. Some are carrying shells and their attitudes express in unique fashion a spirit of life and energy which makes the whole fountain look dynamic, in contrast with the static Tower of Jewels. Everything else in this fountain has the dynamic quality, from its other inhabitants of the lower bowls, those very jolly sea-nymphs, mermaids, or whatever one may want to call them. They are even more fantastically shaped than the larger figures. In their bizarre motives some of the marine mounts look like a cross between a submarine and a rockcod.

Rising from the very center of the fountain basin, a huge sphere, supported by a writhing mass of aquatic beasts, continues the scheme upwards, culminating in the youth on horseback as the dominating figure of the whole scheme. The sphere is charmingly decorated with reclining figures of the two hemispheres and with a great number of minor interesting motives of marine origin. The youth on horseback is not exactly in harmony with the fountain; one feels that the aquatic feeling running through the rest of the fountain is not equally continued in this exceedingly well-modeled horse and youth and those two smaller-scaled figures on his shoulders—I feel that the very clever hand of a most talented artist has not been well supported by a logical idea. Their decorative effect is very marked, taken mainly as a silhouette from a distance. They are no doubt effective in carrying upwards a vertical movement which is to some extent interfered with by the outstretched arms of the youth. Mr. Calder has given us so very many excellent things, alone and in collaboration with others throughout the Exposition, that we must allow him this little bizarre note as an eccentricity of an otherwise well-balanced genius.

As long as we are in the South Gardens, we might take the time to investigate the two fountains on either side of the center, towards the Horticultural Palace on the left and Festival Hall on the right. There we find a very lithe mermaid, used alike on either side, from a model by Arthur Putnam. Many of us who for years looked forward to the great opportunity of the Exposition, which would give Arthur Putnam a worthy field for his great genius, will

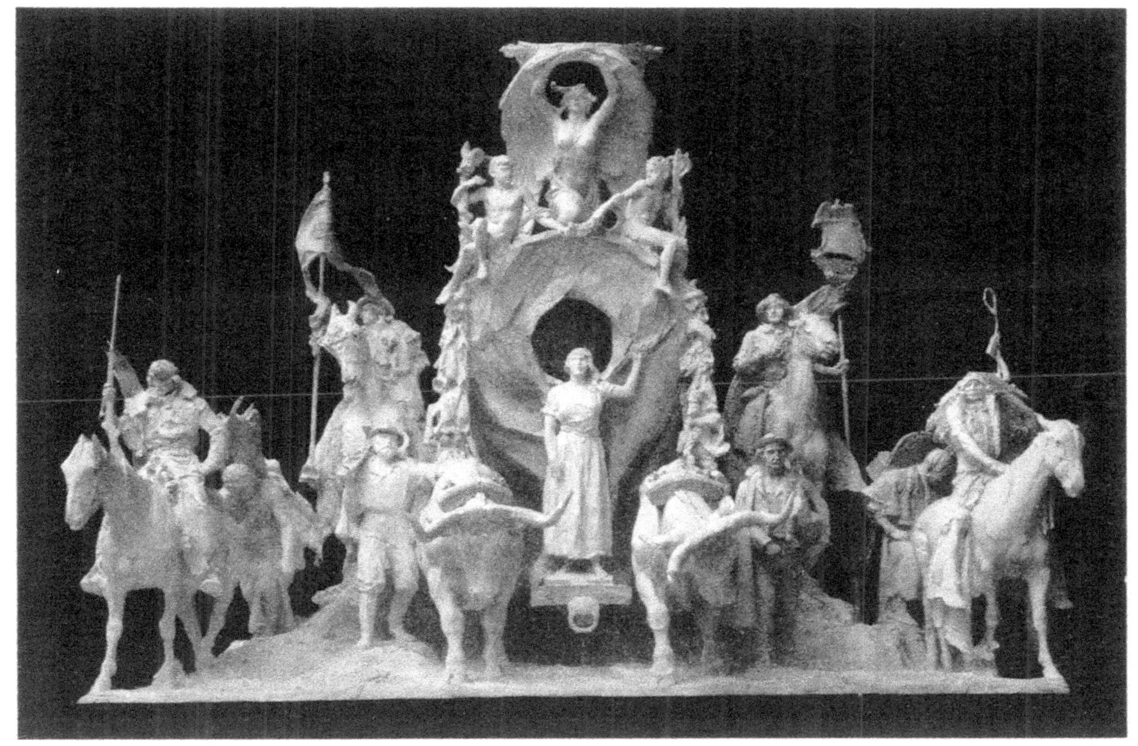

THE NATIONS OF THE WEST
A. STIRLING CALDER, FREDERICK G. R. ROTH, LEO LENTELLI, SCULPTORS

be disappointed to know that the mermaid is his only contribution, and scarcely representative of his original way in dealing with animal forms. The untimely breakdown, some two years ago, of his robust nature prevented his giving himself more typically, for his real spirit is merely suggested in this graceful mermaid.

Sherry Fry's figural compositions on the west of Festival Hall might well be worthy of a little more attention than their somewhat remote location brings them. The two reclining figures on the smaller domes are reposeful and ornate. A stroll through the flower carpets of the South Gardens, amidst the many balustrade lighting Hermae, discloses a wealth of good architectural sculpture, which in its travertine execution is doubly appealing.

There are four equestrian statues in different places on the north side of the Avenue of Palms. Two are in front of the Tower of Jewels, the "Cortez" by Charles Niehaus, and "Pizarro," by Charles Cary Rumsey. The third is in front of the Court of Flowers, and the last at the entrance to the Court of Palms. The two latter, Solon Borglum's "Pioneer," and James Earl Fraser's "The End of the Trail," belong as much together as the two relatively conventional Spanish conquerors guarding the entrance to the Court of the Universe.

The symbolism of the "Pioneer" and "The End of the Trail" is, first of all, a very fine expression of the destinies of two great races so important in our historical development. The erect, energetic, powerful man, head high, with a challenge in his face, looking out into early morning, is very typical of the white man and the victorious march of his civilization. His horse steps lightly, prancingly, and there is admirable expression of physical vigor and hopeful expectation. The gun and axe on his arm are suggestive of his preparedness for any task the day and the future may bring.

Contrast this picture of life with the overwhelming expression of physical fatigue, almost exhaustion, that Fraser gives to his Indian in "The End of the Trail." It is embodied in rider and horse. Man and beast seem both to have reached the end of their resources and both are ready to give up the task they are not equal to meet.

The psychology of this great group is particularly fine. It is in things like these that our American sculpture will yet find its highest expression, rather than in the flamboyant type of technically skillful work so abundantly represented everywhere. "The End of the Trail" could have been placed more effectively in the midst of, or against, groups of shrubbery in a more natural surrounding, where so close a physical inspection as one is invited to in the present location would not be possible.

The Tower of Jewels, however, with its lofty arch and suggestion of hidden things behind it encourages the spirit of investigation. On entering this great arch, one is suddenly attracted by the pleasing sound of two fountains, sheltered in the secluded abutting walls of the great tower. Minor arches, piercing the base of the tower west and east, open up a view toward these sheltered niches, harboring on the right the

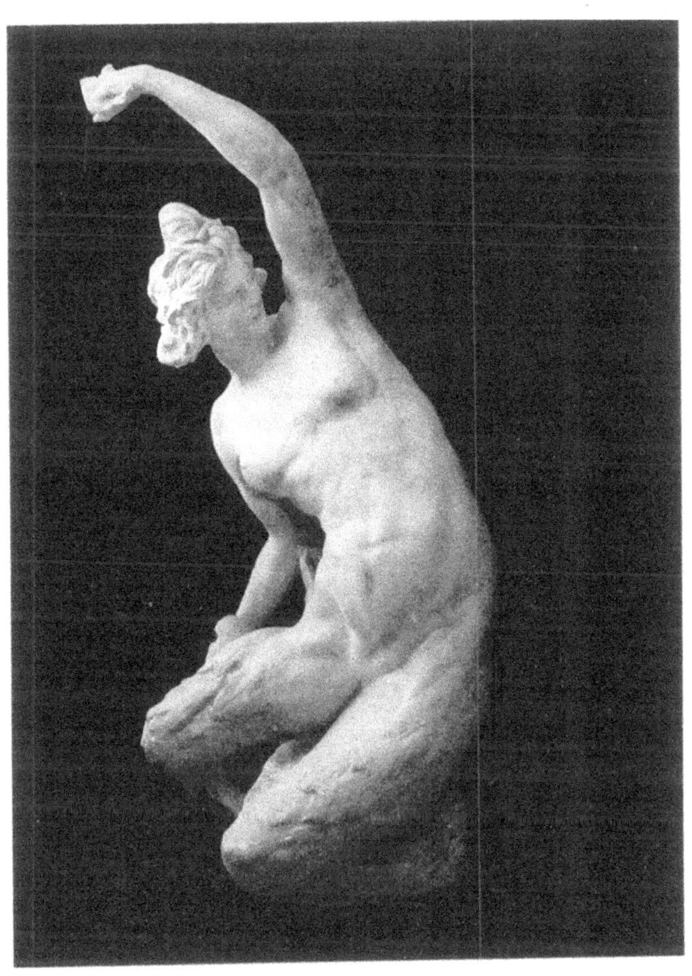

THE MERMAID
ARTHUR PUTNAM, SCULPTOR

Fountain of Youth, by Mrs. Edith Woodman Burroughs, and the Fountain of Eldorado at the left, by Mrs. Harry Payne Whitney. These two fountains are totally different in character, and they could well afford to be so, since they are not visible as a whole at the same time, although physically not far apart.

Mrs. Burrough's fountain is very naïve in feeling, very charming in the graceful modeling of the little girl. The decorative scheme of this poetic unit is very simple and well-sustained throughout its architectural parts.

Mrs. Harry Payne Whitney's fountain is of the intellectual, dramatic kind. The treatment of this almost theatrical subject is well balanced. While it does not possess any too much repose, it is very effective. In general there are three parts to this fountain; the central doorway of Eldorado, just ajar, disclosing faintly this land of happiness; while on either side are two long panels showing great masses of humanity in all manner of positions and attitudes, all striving toward the common goal. Some are shown almost at the end of their journey, overtaken with exhaustion; others more vigorous are lending a willing arm to the support of their less successful brothers and sisters about to fall by the wayside. The whole composition of those two friezes shows Mrs. Whitney as a very skillful and imaginative artist. It is a gratifying spectacle to see a woman such as Mrs. Whitney, so much heralded, possibly against her own inclinations, in the society columns of New York, find the time to devote herself to so serious and professional a piece of work as the Fountain of Eldorado.

Passing through the Tower of Jewels into the Court of the Universe, one's attention will be attracted to a number of pieces of detached statuary. The most important among them is "The Four Elements," by Robert Aitken. We all remember Aitken as the very promising young man who left us before the fire to make a career in the East, after having exhausted all local possibilities, the Bohemian Club included. His figures of the Four Elements are typical of his temperament and he acknowledges in them his indebtedness to Michael Angelo without being in the least imitative. These four figures are allegorically full of meaning, and taken simply as sculpture, they are excellently modeled. His "Fire," showing a Greek warrior defending himself from the fiery breath of a vicious reptile, is novel in its motive, while "Water" discloses Father Neptune bellowing out into the briny air, accompanied by dolphins in rhythmic motions. "Air," on the south, discloses Aitken as the skillful modeler of less muscular forms of a winged female figure, which in itself, without the birds, is suggestive of its meaning. It was very daring to introduce the story of "Icarus" in this group, by the small-scaled figure of this first mythological aviator on the outside of the wings of the larger figure. It helps to add a note of interest to an otherwise not so interesting part of the group.

The Fountains of the Rising and the Setting Sun are most impressive by their architectonic quality, and Weinman's clear style of modeling is seen at its best in the Tritons in the fountain bowl. The figure of the Setting Sun is one of

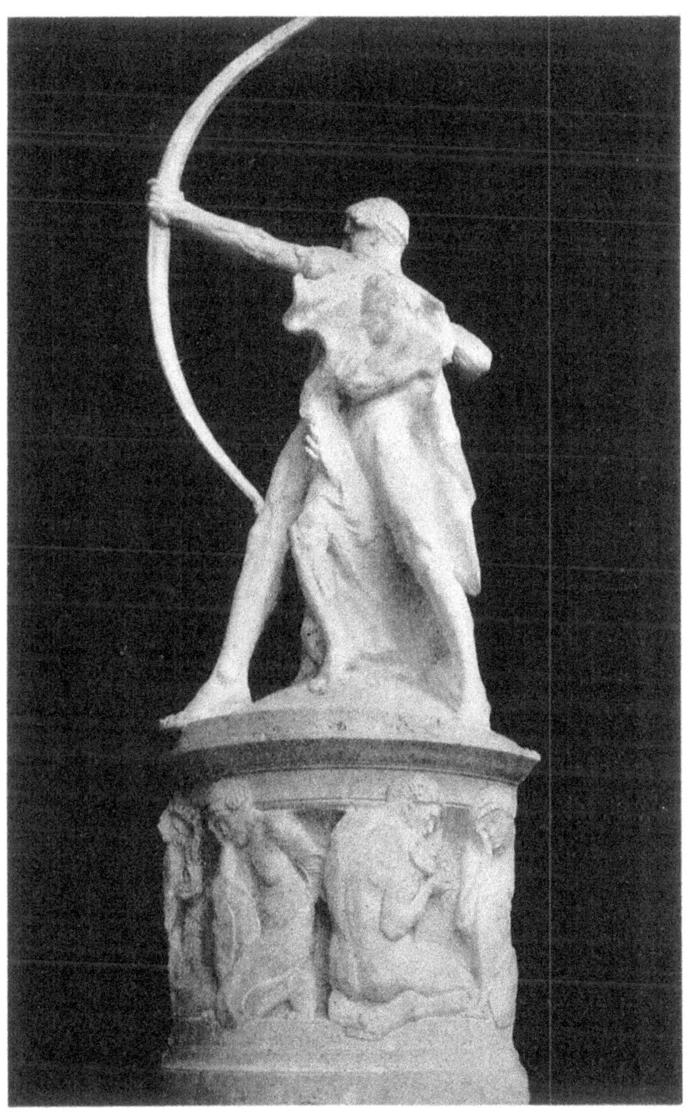

THE ADVENTUROUS BOWMAN SUPPORTED BY FRIEZE OF TOILERS—
DETAILS FROM THE COLUMN OF PROGRESS
HERMON A. MACNEIL, SCULPTOR

the finest figures of the entire Exposition. The suggestion of the termination of day, indicated in the folding of the wings and in the suggestion of physical fatigue, is very well conveyed. A fine relaxation runs through the whole figure.

The Rising Sun, on the other side, has all the buoyancy of an energetic youth ready for his daily task. With widespread wings, looking squarely out into the world, he seems ready to soar into the firmament. The contrast is admirable in these two figures, and Weinman deserves all the popular applause bestowed upon his work.

Paul Manship has contributed two groups at the head of the east and west steps leading to the sunken gardens, each group consisting of two figures, one representing Festivity, the other, Art and Music. These groups are used alike on either side. Manship deserves to be better represented in the Exposition than by these two groups alone. His position as one of the very successful of our younger men would have warranted a more extensive employment of his very strong talent.

It is rather a flight from those Manship figures to the colossal groups of the Nations of the East and of the West, but one is irresistibly drawn to these wonderfully effective compositions. Their location makes them the most prominent groups in the Exposition ensemble.

The harmonious co-operation of Calder, Roth, and Lentelli has resulted in the creation of a modern substitute for the old Roman quadriga, which so generally crowns triumphal arches. Both groups are so skillfully composed as to have a similar silhouette against the blue sky, but individually considered they are full of a great variety of detail. It was an accomplishment to balance the huge bulk of an elephant by a prairie schooner on the opposite side of the court. Considering the almost painful simplicity of the costumes and general detail of the western nations as contrasted with the elaborately decorative accessories, trappings, and tinsel of the Orient, it was no small task to produce a feeling of balance between these two foreign motives. But what it lacked in that regard was made up by allegorical figures, like those on top of the prairie schooner, used not so much to express an idea as to fill out the space occupied by the howdah on the other side. There is a great deal of fine modeling in the individual figures on horse and camel back and on foot.

In either one of the two groups much has been lost in the great height of the arches. Figures like "The Alaskan," "The Trapper," and "The Indian," for instance, are particularly fine and they would be very effective by themselves. "The Mother of Tomorrow" in the Nations of the West is a beautifully simple piece of sculpture.

The Nations of the East, like the West, in its entirety, is the conception of A. Stirling Calder, who modeled the pedestrian figures. With Mr. Calder, Messrs. Frederick G. R. Roth and Leo Lentelli collaborated. The huge elephant in the center of the group was modeled by Mr. Roth, also the camels. The mounted horsemen were modeled by Leo Lentelli. From left to right the figures are—an Arab warrior, a Negro servitor bearing baskets of fruit, a camel

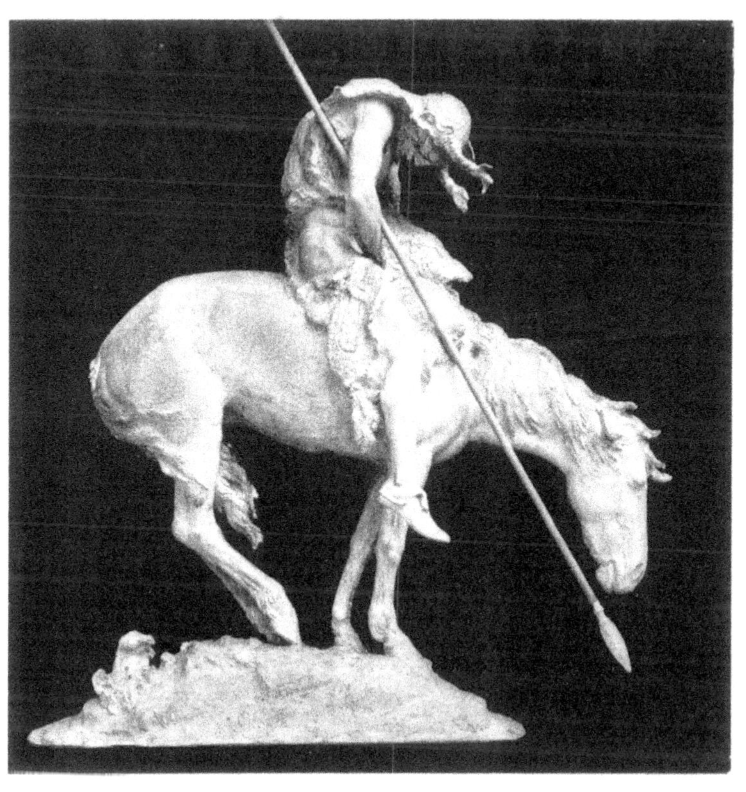

THE END OF THE TRAIL
JAMES EARL FRASER, SCULPTOR

and rider (the Egyptian), a falconer, an elephant with a howdah containing a figure embodying the spirit of the East, attended by Oriental mystics representing India, a Buddhist Lama bearing his emblem of authority, a camel and rider (Mahometan), a Negro servitor, and a Mongolian warrior. The size of the group, crowning a triumphal arch one hundred and sixty feet in height, may be inferred from the fact that the figure of the Negro servitor is thirteen feet six inches in height.

On the arch beneath this group are inscribed these lines by Kalidasa: "The moon sinks yonder in the west, while in the east the glorious sun behind the herald dawn appears. Thus rise and set in constant change those shining orbs and regulate the very life of this our world."

The Nations of the West, crowning the arch of the Setting Sun, is also the conception of A. Stirling Calder, who modeled the imaginative figures of "the Mother of Tomorrow," "Enterprise," and "Hopes of the Future." Messrs. Leo Lentelli and Frederick G. R. Roth collaborated in their happiest style, the former producing the four horsemen and one pedestrian, the Squaw, and the latter the oxen, the wagon, and the three pedestrians. From left to right the figures are, the French Trapper, the Alaskan, the Latin-American, the German, the Hopes of the Future (a white boy and a Negro, riding on a wagon), Enterprise, the Mother of Tomorrow, the Italian, the Anglo-American, the Squaw, the American Indian. The group is is conceived in the same large monumental style as the Nations of the East. The types of those colonizing nations that at one time or place or another have left their stamp on our country have been selected to form the composition.

The following lines by Walt Whitman are inscribed on the arch beneath the group of the Nations of the West: "Facing west from California's shores, inquiring, tireless, seeking what is yet unfound, I a child, very old, over waves towards the house of maternity, the land of migrations, look afar: look off the shores of my western sea, the circle almost circled."

It is popularly conceded that these two groups are magnificently daring conceptions, richly worked out. They are probably the largest groups of the kind ever made, the dimensions of the base being fifty-two by thirty-eight feet, and the height forty-two feet.

Looking seaward from the Court of the Universe the Column of Progress commands attention, crowned by the "Adventurous Bowman" and decorated at the base with a frieze symbolizing achievement, or progress. The very fine symbolism in this column deserves to be studied. The position of the column itself is most artistic in its relation to the surroundings. It is too bad, however, to see the view from the main court toward the column spoiled by a music pavilion of dubious architectural merit. The effect of the column as seen from any point is inspiring in its monumental grandeur. The group on top, the Bowman, represents man's supreme effort in life. He is supported on the left by his fellow-man, adding strength and steadiness to his aim, while on the right the

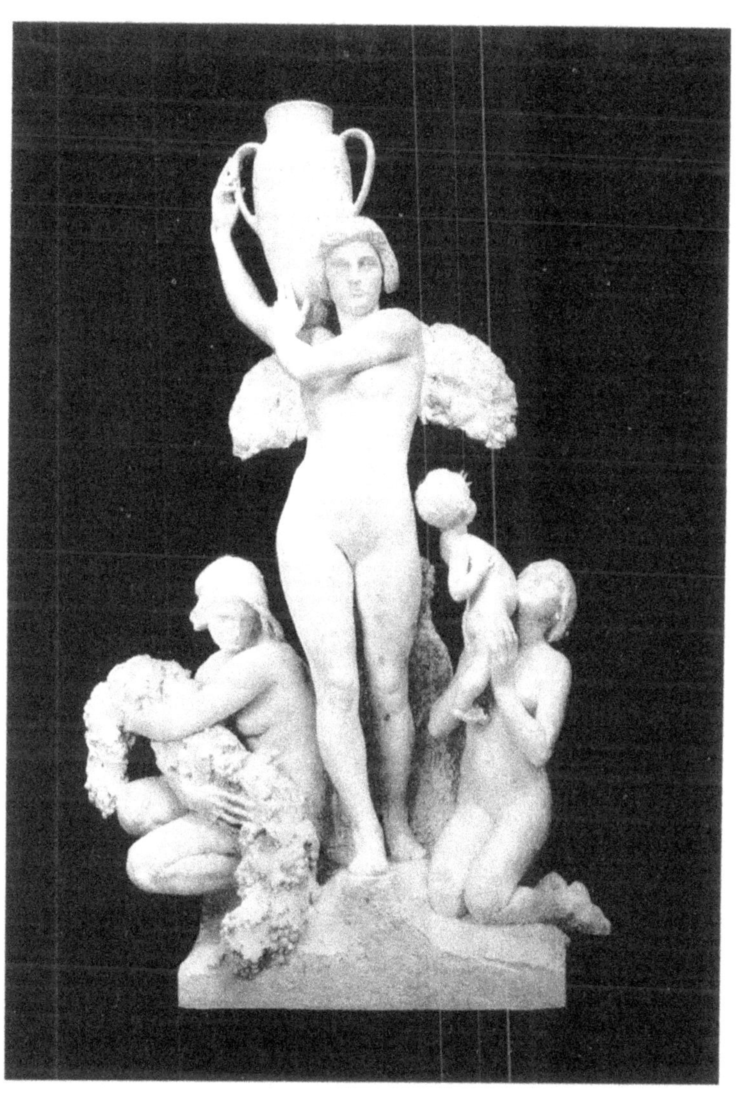

AUTUMN, IN THE COURT OF THE FOUR SEASONS
FURIO PICCIRILLI, SCULPTOR

crouching figure of a woman watches anxiously the sureness of his aim. She holds ready in her hand the laurel wreath which she confidently feels will be his just reward.

The great Column of Progress is the first column in the world, so far as I know, whose design was inspired by a purely imaginative motive, and the first sculpture column at any exposition. It must be considered the most splendid expression of sculpture and architectural art in the Exposition. Mr. Calder may justly feel proud of this great idea and Mr. Hermon MacNeil has added new laurels to his many accomplishments in the free modeling of the very daring group on top.

The column itself is decorated with the spiral ascending motive of the Ship of Life, while at the base Isadore Konti expresses the striving for achievement in four well modeled panels of huge scale, representing human life in its progressive stages, showing men and women in attitudes of hope and despair, of strength and weakness, in the never ending task of trying to realize human destiny.

The Court of the Four Seasons harbors four groups by Piccirilli, representing the seasons in the conventional way, dividing the year into four distinct parts—spring, summer, autumn, and winter. These four groups of Piccirilli are not equally successful. By far the most effective is the one representing winter. The severe rigidity of the lovely central standing figure expresses well that feeling of suspended activity which we associate with the conventional conceptions of the season of dormant life. The kneeling side figures are in full harmony of expression with the central figure. They support very well the general scheme.

The next best, to my mind, seems "Spring," on account of the very fine psychological quality of the standing figure in giving expression in a very graceful fashion to that invigorating and reviving quality of our loveliest season. The two side figures seem to be gradually awakening to the full development of their powers.

Next to "Spring," "Fall," by the fullness of the decorative scheme, suggests Peace and Plenty in the preparation for the Harvest Festival and in the touch of family life of the mother and child on the right.

Mr. Piccirilli's naturalistic modeling does not express itself so well in "Summer." There is so little strictly architectural feeling in that group. I think that Albert Jaegers, with his two single figures on top of the two columns flanking the Orchestral Niche, actually represents our own two seasons much more successfully than does Piccirilli. Jaegers' "Rain and Sunshine" should be used to name the court properly—"The Court of the Two Seasons," as we know them in California—the dry season, the season of harvest; and the wet season, the one of recuperation. I regret that here an opportunity was lost to add distinction to the many different features of a great undertaking.

Jaegers has contributed also the figure of "Nature" on top of the music niche and the capital bulls on the pylons toward the north of the court. These terra cotta bulls are surely worthy of the adjective derived from them.

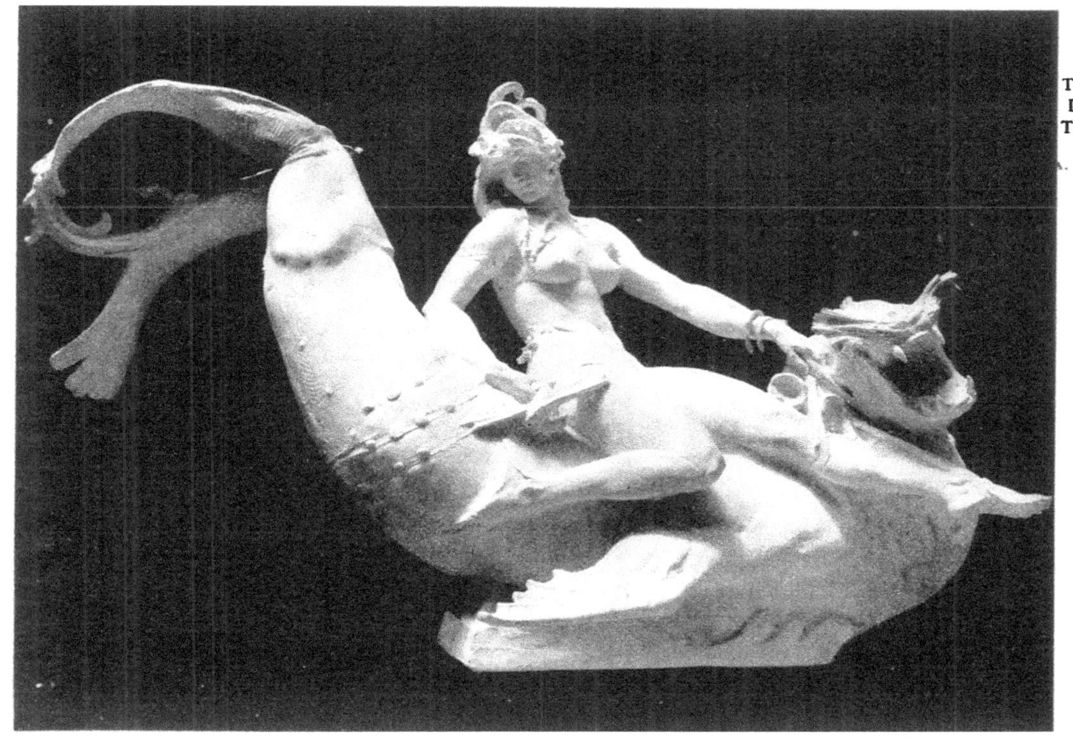

THE PACIFIC —
DETAIL FROM
THE FOUNTAIN
OF ENERGY
A. STIRLING CALDER,
SCULPTOR

Their relative size is very good, and to see them in the richness of their color against the upper regions of a dark blue sky is very effective.

Directly north of the Court of the Four Seasons stands Miss Beatrice Evelyn Longman's Fountain of Ceres, originally planned for the center of the court, but so very effective all by itself between the dignified colonnades of the avenue. The fountain is most impressive by its fine architectural feeling, so uncommon in the work of many women sculptors. The general feeling of it is refinement, combined with great strength. It is fully deserving of monopolizing a fine setting of dignified architecture, so richly emphasized by some of the finest old yew trees in the grounds.

In the Court of Abundance a riot of interesting architectural sculptural details invites the attention of the visitor. Beginning with the lower animal forms, such as crabs and crayfish, etc., the entire evolution of Nature has been symbolized, reaching its climax in the tower, where the scheme is continued in several groups in Chester Beach's best style. The lowest of these groups shows the Primitive Age, followed above by the Middle Ages and Modernity. The great charm of this finest of all the towers in the Exposition is its wonderful rhythmic feeling. The graceful flow of line from the base toward the top is never interrupted, in spite of the many sculptural adornments used on all sides. In front of the tower are two very ornate illuminating shafts, showing Leo Lentelli's diabolical cleverness in making ornament out of human figures. Leo Lentelli's style is particularly well adapted to Mullgardt's Court of Abundance. Its care-free, subtle quality, full of animation, presenting new motives at every turn, is most helpful in the general spirit of festivity which characterizes this most interesting of all the courts.

Aitken's Fountain of Life in the center of the court is totally different. Full of intellectual suggestion, it is almost bewildering in the story-telling quality of its many details. Aitken's fountain, which is situated in the center of a basin a hundred and fifty feet long by sixty-five feet wide, rises directly from the water. The main structure consists of a series of four groups of heroic-sized figures, carved in pierced relief, each flanked by colossal bronze Hermes, their arms reaching around the structure and held together by animal forms of reptilian or fishy origin. All these forms and figures surround a globe of enormous size, typifying the Earth, over the surface of which streams of water are thrown from the reptilian chain motive.

Leading up to the main structure is a group of ten crouching figures, symbolizing Destiny in the shape of two enormous arms and hands, giving life with one and taking it with the other. Here, on the left side, are arranged figures suggesting the Dawn of Life, while on the right are men and women depicting the fullness and the end of existence.

In the first, Prenatal Sleep, is the crouched form of a woman, while successively come the Awakening, the Ecstatic Joy of Being—or it may be the Realization of Living; the Kiss of Life, with the human pair offering up their

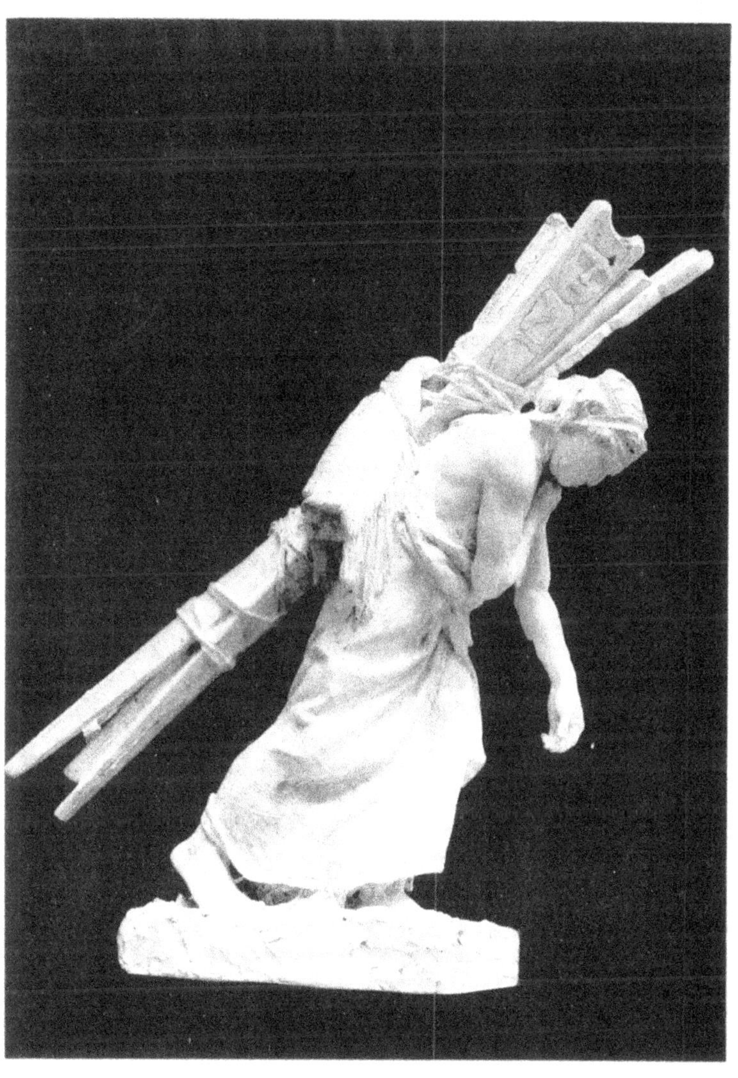

THE ALASKAN — DETAIL FROM NATIONS OF THE WEST
FREDERICK G. R. ROTH, SCULPTOR

children, representative of the beginnings of fecundity; a female, strong of limb and superb of physique, enfolds in her arms two infants, while her mate, of no less powerful build and rude force, kneeling beside her, gives her an embrace typical of the overpowering parental instinct. Here is the suggestion of the elemental feelings, the beginnings of things.

Between the first group and the central one comes a gap, a space typical of that unknown time in history when conjecture alone permits speculation, and the story is taken up again with the first of the central groups, wherein stands a figure of Vanity, glass in hand, symbolizing the compelling motive of so much in human endeavor. To her left, in enormous contrast, are primitive man and woman, treated with great realism, these two carrying their burdens of life, in the form of their progeny, into the unknown future, their expression that of rude but questioning courage, the man splendid in his virility, superb in the attitude of his awkward strength, ready to meet whatever be the call of earth. His mate meanwhile suggests the overwhelming and eternal instincts of motherhood.

An archaic Hermes, dividing these figures from the next group, allows for a space of time to elapse, and we come to their children, now grown to manhood and womanhood, in their rude strength finding themselves, with the result of Natural Selection. This is a group of five personages, the center figure a man of splendid youth and vigor, suggesting the high state both of physical and intellectual perfection, unconsciously attracting the female, two of whom regard him with favor, while two males on either side, deserted for this finer type, give vent to deep regret, despair, and anger. One attempts by brute force to hold the woman; the other reluctantly gives up his choice, in the obvious futility of his unequal intellectual endowment to comprehend.

From this to the Survival of the Fittest we have a militant group, in which physical strength begins to play its part, and perhaps discloses the first awakening of the war spirit, the woman in this case being the exciting cause. The powerful chieftains struggle for supremacy of their time and tribe, their women making futile efforts to separate them. Here the sense of conquest receives its first impression and is finely indicated, with admirable action, while there is the symbolism of the conflict of the nations that has ever gone on, for one cause or another, and that struggle for the female which has ever been the actuating motive in war, conquest, and, for that matter, peace.

The next group—always separated by the solemn and dignified Hermae—discloses "The Lesson of Life," wherein the elders, with the experience of the years, offer to hot-headed youth and to the lovelorn the benefit of their own trials and struggles. A beautiful woman is the central figure. She draws to her side splendid manhood, the Warrior, willing to fight for his love and his faith. To his left his mother offers him her affectionate advice, while to the right a father restrains a wayward offspring who, rejected by the female, is in a state of frenzied

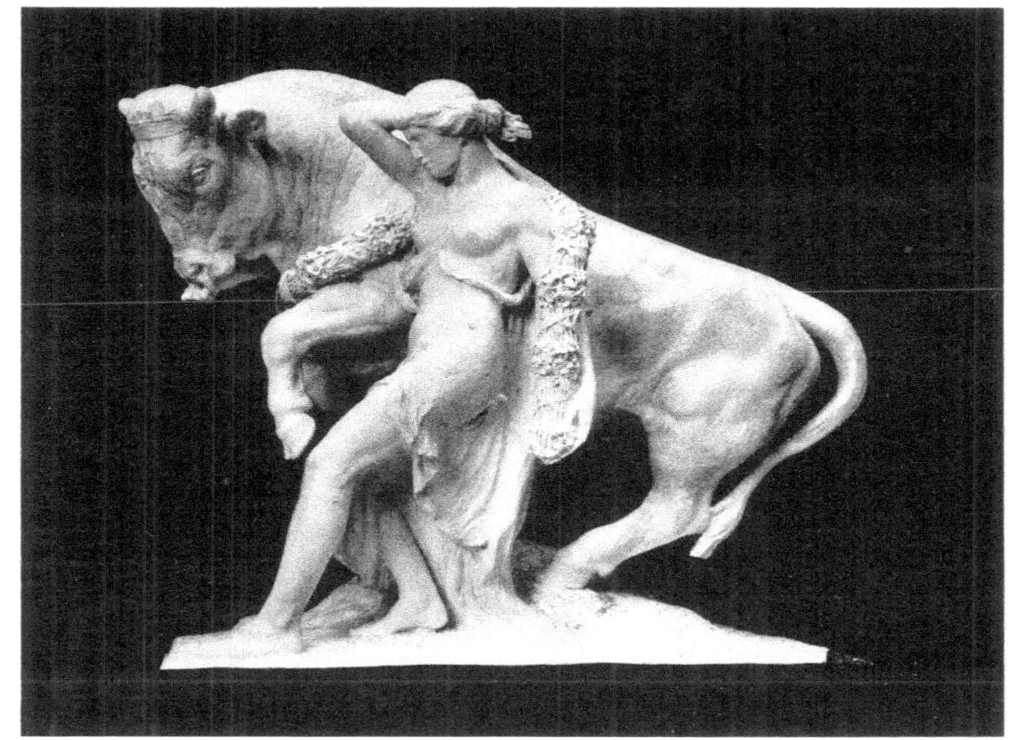

THE FEAST OF SACRIFICE
ALBERT JAEGERS, SCULPTOR

jealousy. Finally two figures represent Lust, a man struggling to caress the unwilling woman who shrinks from his embraces, and we are led down from this pair out of the composition to the crouching group at the approach of the structure, referred to at the beginning of this description, who here are departing from the central composition.

First is a figure of Greed looking back on the Earth. He holds in his hands a mass suggestive of his futile and unsavory worldly possessions, the unworthy bauble toward which his efforts have been directed. Back of him we have the group of Faith, wherein kneels a Patriarch, who offers consolation to a woman to whom he presents the hope of immortality, holding in his hands a scarab, ancient symbol of renewed life. Next come two recumbent figures, a man and a woman, the first, Sorrow, the other typifying Final Slumber. These are about to be drawn into oblivion by the relentless hand of Destiny.

In the center of a formal parapet at the end of the basin of water, sixty feet from the fountain, is a colossal figure symbolic of the setting sun, Helios, the great orb having thrown off the nebulous mass that subsequently resolved itself into the earth.

In the immediate neighborhood of this Court of Abundance is found Sherry Fry's figure of Neptune's Daughter, in the open court north of the tower. The figure is not in keeping with the scheme of Mullgardt's court, extending in this direction. The effect of this figure, no matter how graceful it may be, is unquestionably too physical, in a certain measure owing to the opportunity for close inspection.

On the south of the Court of Abundance, in the Court of Flowers, Edgar Walter's fountain has been placed. "Beauty and the Beast" have been combined in contrasting fashion, with much effect, by associating the youthful charms of a graceful maid with the angular ugliness of a dragon, who seems to feel honored by having been selected as the resting-place of a creature from outside his realm. He seems to be almost hypnotized into a state of abject lifelessness. The effect of this juxtaposition of the round forms of the human body and the almost geometrical angularity of the fabulous beast is very interesting and adds a new note to the many other ideas presented. The architectural scheme of the fountain is made doubly interesting by a rich use of animal forms of humorous character.

The immediate vicinity of the Laguna remains still to be investigated in regard to sculptural adornments. The dozen or so niches in the west front of the main building present a repetition of two individual groups by Charles Harley, of New York, of decidedly archaeological character—"The Triumph of the Field" and "Abundance." They are most serious pieces of work, possibly too serious, and they are in great danger of remaining caviar to the masses on account of the complexity of their symbolism and the intellectual character of their motives. Their setting is most atractive, amongst groups of trees and shrubs.

Maybeck's Palace of Fine Arts is so overwhelming in its architectural effects that one seldom feels like doing justice to the fine sculptural detail everywhere in this building. Ralph

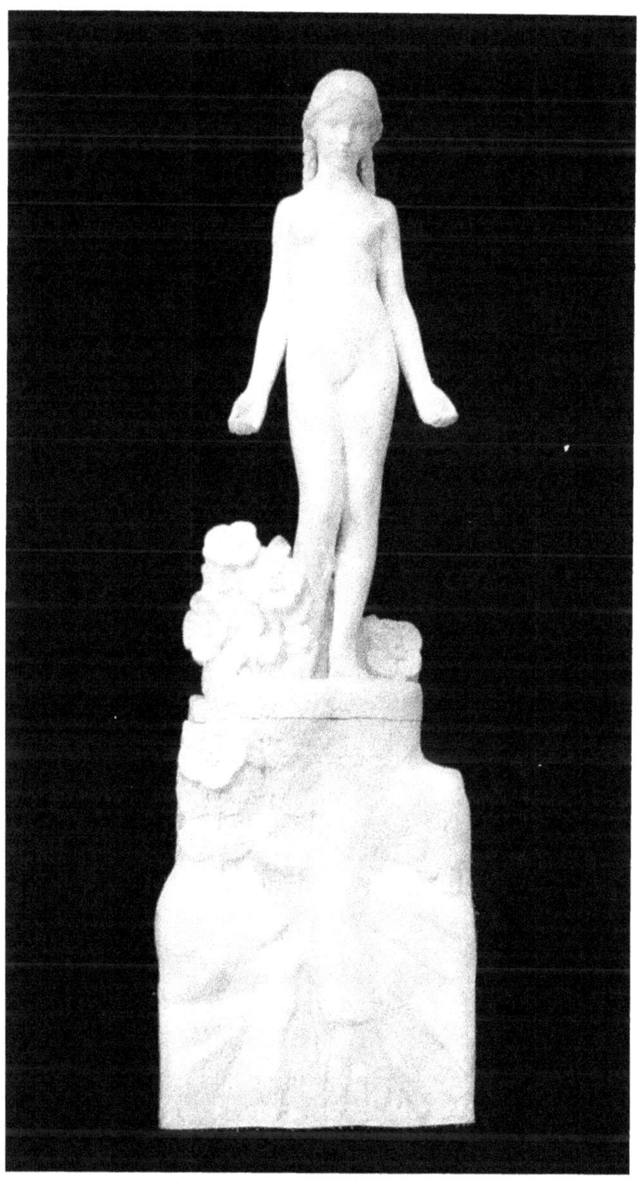

YOUTH — FROM THE FOUNTAIN OF YOUTH
EDITH WOODMAN BURROUGHS, SCULPTOR

Stackpole's interesting Shrine of Inspiration is the most charming bit of sculpture, more detached in its effect than most of the other motives. Bruno Zimm's eight fine friezes, showing the development and influences of the arts in a very severe, almost archaic style of modeling, add a fine note to the dome, and Ulric Ellerhusen's equally architectonic friezes are in good style and are in thorough harmony with the classic quality of this great palace.

It is, of course, not possible to name all of the many pieces of architectural sculpture used at the Exposition. The general effect one receives is that it represents the best that is possible in Exposition sculpture today. It gives evidence of the increasing development of the qualities of design, as contrasted with the so much looser work of former expositions. Seldom before have sculptors anywhere, since sculpture and architecture first worked hand in hand, so played their most important roles together in the ensemble setting that constitutes our Exposition visually. On arch or column, in niches, in fountains, and in free-standing groups, they sing of many themes, and always in harmony, but with no loss of character or individuality. There is no doubt of it, that, for an Exposition, sculpture is the most important of all the arts, because it is the most human. Without it, architecture would be cold and without appeal. I foresee a great future for sculpture in America, where our temperament demands it. The educational value of sculpture at an exposition is incalculable. It is a school for the sculptors, too, as well as for the public.

THE COLOR SCHEME & LANDSCAPE GARDENING

NOTHING excites the Exposition visitor more than the color scheme of the buildings. But "excite" is really not the proper word, because there is nothing exciting about it. Nothing was farther from Mr. Guérin's mind than to create excitement, unrest, or any of those sensations that might lead to fatigue or even to a nervous breakdown. We understand fully by this time that it was Jules Guérin who is the responsible artist, and who supervised the putting into existence of the first real "Guérin" that ever was. Mr. Guérin has the distinction of being the first director of color and of decoration ever appointed for an international exposition.

It must become evident to any person who is at all familiar with the fascinating tonal designs Guérin produces for many of our leading magazines that what he did was nothing but to paint nature as he has been used to represent it in his pictures. Guérin must have had a glorious time with that first great opportunity, so seldom to happen, of putting all those pet colors of his into the actual outdoors, there to feast his eyes upon them. It was a daring and novel undertaking, most successful in a large way. I hope

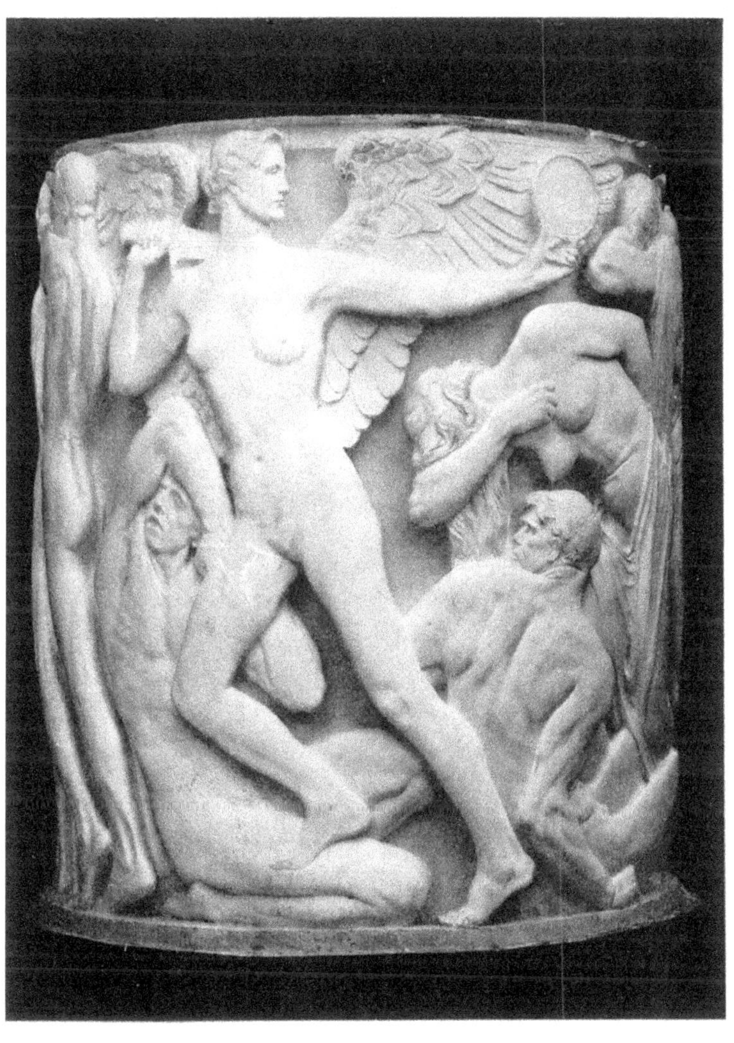

TRUTH — DETAIL FROM THE FOUNTAIN OF THE RISING SUN
ADOLPH A. WEINMAN SCULPTOR

we are going to benefit by this successful experiment and begin to give life to our dreary cement façades, mournful roofs, and lifeless window-sashes, ornamentations, and what not. We are, I admit, hopelessly at the mercy of the house-painter, who knows much about estimates, something about paint, and little about color. I hope we are going to learn the difference between paint and color, the purely physical, meaningless thing on the one hand, and the intelligence-conveying, pleasure-giving element on the other.

Guérin certainly knows color, and I take it for granted that a man of his training and experience knows how to use paint. His exposition buildings look for all the world like a live Guérin print taken from the Century Magazine and put down alongside of the bay which seems to have responded, as have the other natural assets, for a blending of the entire creation into one harmonious unit. I fancy such a thing was possible only in California, where natural conditions invite such a technical and artistic innovation.

The general effect is one of great warmth. The basic tone of the travertine furnishes a very rich foundation for the other colors added. The whole range of color is very simple and it is simplicity and repetition over large areas that make the colors so effective. There are three different greens, for instance—the patina green on many minor domes, suggesting aged copper surfaces; a very strong primary green, on the small doors of the palaces and most of the lattice work; and another very pale, pinkish green, a sort of an abalone shell green, used on all the flagpole bases, always topped off with a light pinkish red, used above the light green base on all the flagpoles.

Then there are the reds, a number of different reds, running from a pinkish brick color to a darker russet red, to be found exclusively in all vertical panels serving as background for detailed statuary—for instance, in all the courts. Next to the red there is a brilliant orange, used in relatively small quantities here and there in the mouldings, as around the Brangwyn paintings in the Court of Abundance.

This leaves yet to be named the few soothing blues that abound in the ceilings, in the deep recesses of the walls, and the coffered arches, serving as backgrounds for the many richly-modeled terra cotta rosettes.

This is practically the entire range of colors, but they assume, of course, endless variations of tone and intensity, owing to the difference of the surfaces and the play of light and shadow. The relation of the whole color scheme to the colors furnished by nature is by no means accidental. The effect of the ensemble, on a calm, sunny day, is hard to describe in its gorgeous beauty.

The pressing into service of nature as applied to color was particularly inviting, of course, on the bay side, where simple sweeps of skies, foothills, and plain bodies of water furnish almost ideal conditions. This is true in a similar way for the background in the west, but toward the south—well, we had better forget such mournful outward aspects of our great city of San

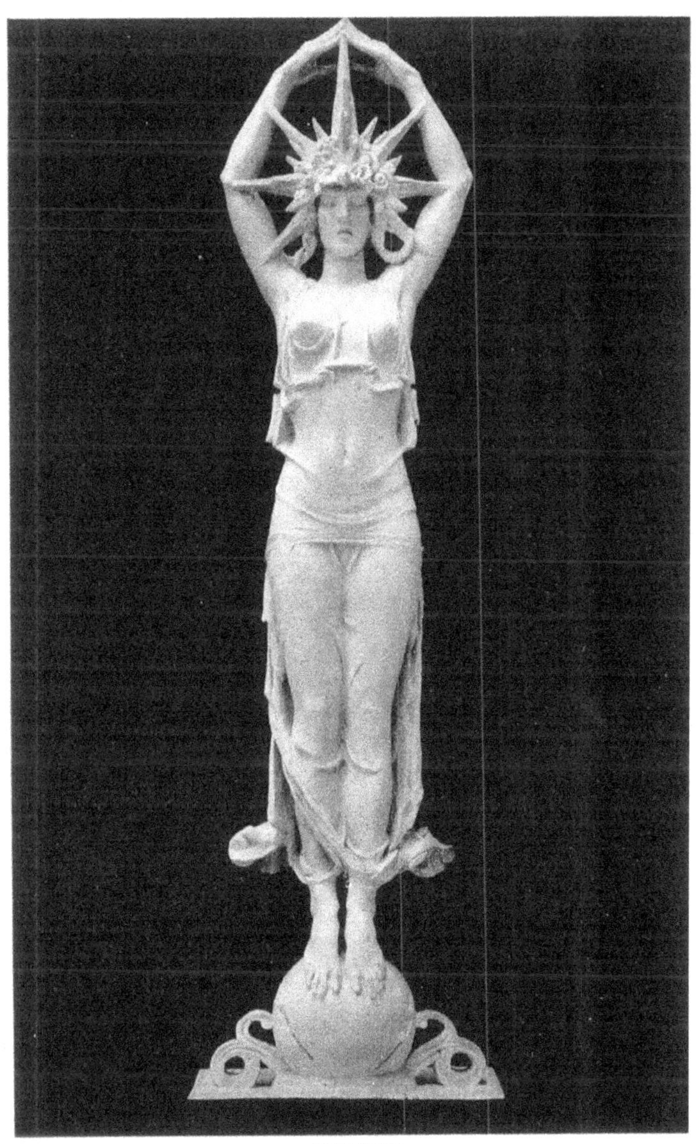

THE STAR
A. STIRLING CALDER, SCULPTOR

Francisco, known around the world for its gay temperament.

Appreciating the importance of detail, Guérin extended his color treatment to practically everything presenting surface. Nothing could escape his vigilant eyes. Even the sand covering of the asphalted roads is of a peculiarly attractive blend. It seems like a mixture of ordinary sand with a touch of cinnamon. Even that corps of stalwart guards had to submit to a tonal harmony of drabs, with touches of yellow metal, warm red puttees, and neat little yellow Spanish canes. They all seem very proud and appreciative of their part in the concert of colors. and they speak of it with feeling and reverence. Not long ago, during a rather stormy, wet day, I happened to notice several of these cicerones hiding in a doorway of one of the palaces, looking most disconsolate. The reason for it became immediately apparent; the un-Californian weather had forced them to put on civilian overcoats of indescribable hues, and the shame of being out of color was plainly written in their faces. It shows that art is largely a matter of education.

I fancy that all that a respectful and appreciative public could do, in order to live up to the occasion, would be to have Exposition suits built of pongee silk, or some other harmonious material. So far, on all of my visits, I observed a shocking preponderance of black, which I hope will eventually yield to the softer colors of lighter materials, with the arrival of warmer weather.

The careful observer will find that the crimson vermilion red of the fire alarm boxes had to yield to a more refined vivid orange, much, I understand, to the consternation of the Exposition fire marshal, who must have been shocked at this intrusion.

The horticultural effect of the grounds, flower beds, and shrubbery will always adapt itself properly to the color scheme, and a preponderance of warm yellows, reds, and orange will simultaneously fill out the garden areas. At first yellow pansies and daffodils had control, to be replaced in due season by the uniform appearance of tulips, hyacinths, and successions of other flowers. This progressive appearance of new flower carpets will provide ever-changing elements of interest throughout the entire period of the Exposition.

It seems only right at this time to speak of the great and modestly contributed services of John McLaren. He, with his wide experience and unceasing energy, created the garden setting which ties all the buildings into a natural harmony. Hardly ever have trees, shrubs, and flowers been used in such profusion in an Exposition. Conventional in aspect, all great expositions in the past have been lacking in the invigorating elements, no matter how naturalistic the site may have been. The few scraggly pines of St. Louis looked more like undesirable left-overs of a former forest than like a supporting feature of the Exposition picture.

The stony look of many former expositions is not evident at San Francisco. Considering the fact that the exposition is largely on made ground, it is amazing what has been accomplished. With the exception of the few scat-

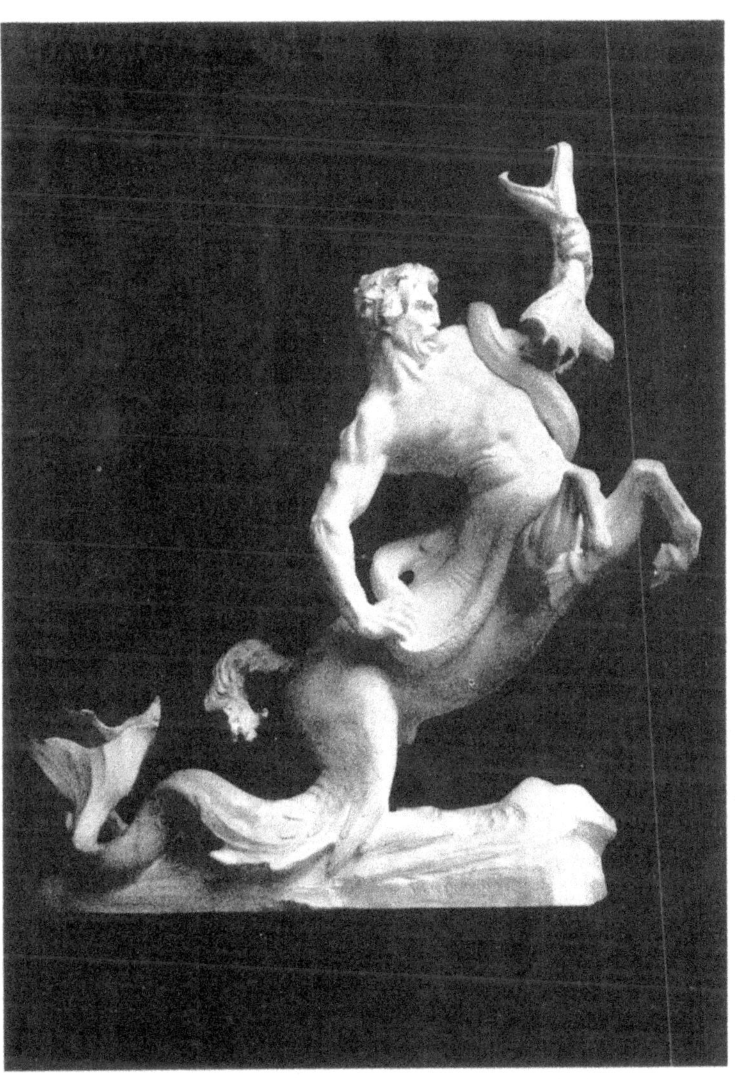

THE TRITON — DETAIL OF THE FOUNTAINS OF THE RISING AND THE SETTING SUN

ADOLPH A. WEINMAN, SCULPTOR

tering remains of an old amusement park—the Harbor View Gardens—so charmingly utilized in the courtyard of the California building, practically all the trees and shrubs had to be brought in from the outside. How well Mr. McLaren succeeded in moving whole gardens "en bloc" to the Exposition is shown by the fact that with the exception of a few Monterey cypresses on one of the lagoon islands, not a single tree has died. It was no small task to transplant eucalypti forty feet high, and aged yew trees, and the tradition that it is impossible to transplant old trees has again been demonstrated as in the same class with other old sayings based on the experience of the past, but applying no longer to our own conditions.

The stately rows of palms on the south avenue contain some specimens of the Canary Island palms which must be nearly forty years old, and some of the yews in the colonnade between the Court of the Four Seasons and the Marina, near Miss Longman's Fountain of Ceres, are probably even older. The massing of large groups of black acacia, Monterey pines, and cypresses, filled in at the edge with veronica and many other flowering shrubs, gives many interesting notes, and serves frequently as backgrounds for statuary.

Like everything else, from the architecture down, the garden aspect of the Exposition is not frugal nor skimpy, whatever floral effects are used. Like shrubbery, trees occur in great profusion, and without regard for difficulties in transplanting.

The Court of the Universe did not receive the generous treatment from Mr. McLaren that it almost cries for. The few isolated Italian cypresses in the Court, near the tower, no doubt help a good deal, but one is tempted to ask why there are not more of them. Italian cypresses are hard to transplant, particularly if their feet have become accustomed to the peaceful conditions of Santa Clara Valley cemeteries, where most of them, I understand, enjoyed an undisturbed existence until they were used so very effectively in the Exposition. These successfully moved old trees are by far the most useful trees in architectural schemes, as anybody who knows the Villa Borghese in Rome must admit.

I would like to see a law passed that every person at a certain age must plant six Italian cypresses. I humbly suggest this to our legislators, who seem to be suffering from a lack of measures to be introduced and passed for the benefit of the people.

The Italian cypress is our most picturesque tree, and for combination with architecture, is unrivaled by any other tree. They grow rather slowly, but do not take much space, on account of their vertical habit. The making of the Court of Palms is due largely to the liberal use of these elegant trees, with their somber stateliness.

The lover of outdoors will find no end to his pleasurable investigations in the many fine, luxurious groupings of flowering shrubs. Heather, which does so well with us, and blooms when only few flowers brighten our gardens, has been profusely used in solid beds at the base of the Kelham towers, around Festival Hall, and in many

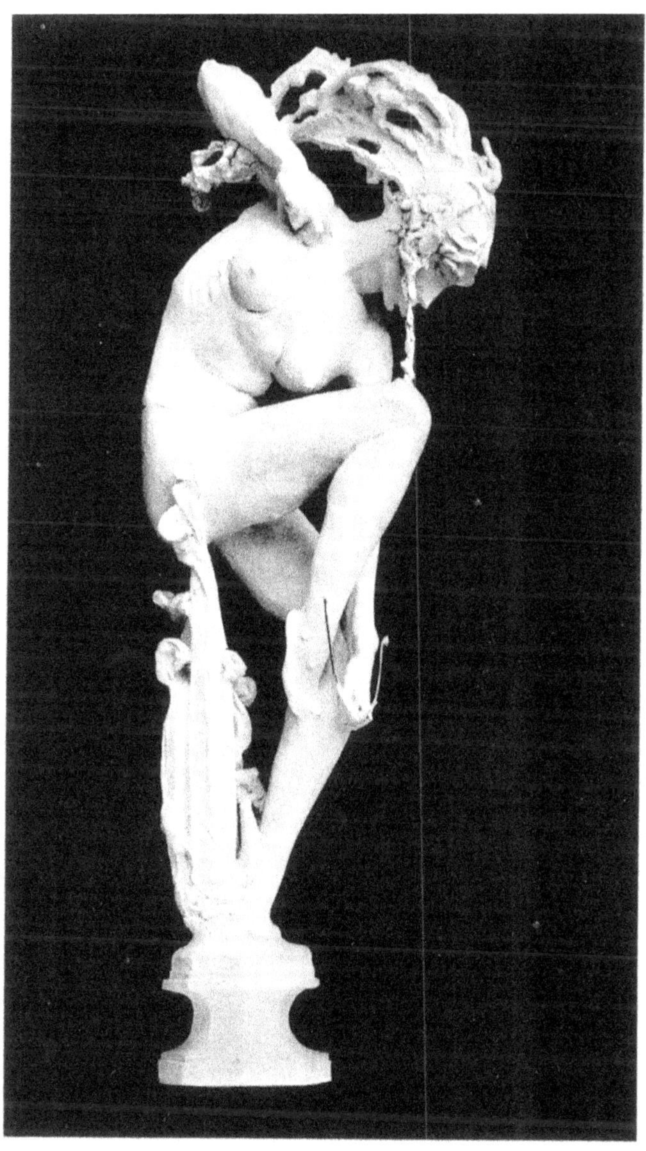

FINIAL FIGURE IN THE COURT OF ABUNDANCE
LEO LENTELLI, SCULPTOR

other places. The dainty, glistening foliage, interspersed with red berries of another acclimated alien from the Himalaya Mountains—the Cotoneaster—makes fine borders around the pool in the Court of the Four Seasons, in the Court of Palms, and in several of the colonnades.

Evergreen plants and shrubs are the dominant features of the two Italian Avenues connecting the big court with the side courts. The rich and luxuriant carpets of the many varieties of box, thuya, taxus, and dwarf pine, in dark, somber greens and many lighter color variations, are superb.

In the Court of Abundance great masses of orange trees furnish the dominant note. They are most effective with their branches heavily laden with fruit. They are not only a surprise to the outsider, but even to the Californian, who wonders at the skill and experience which made this feat possible.

MURAL DECORATIONS

In connection with the color scheme, the mural decorations invite attention at many places. The outdoor character of the Exposition has given unusual locations to some of these decorations. There are in all some thirty. Mr. Guérin, as the director of color, had full charge of their production, and all of them were painted by men he trusted personally as regards their ability to execute and to finish on time. That his choice fell largely on Eastern men was only too natural.

Few people have a proper idea of the magnitude of the work involved in painting a huge decoration, and Mr. Guérin can hardly be blamed for his choice of the men of experience who finally did the work, although not all of them justified the confidence placed in them. The work of painting such huge decorations is necessarily a big undertaking, involving many preliminary studies and much physical and mechanical labor in the end. Many painter-decorators employ large numbers of trained men, apprentices and independent artists, to assist in the execution of their commissions, and very frequently the temptation of yielding the pleasure of execution to other hands is the cause of the lowering of standards.

Probably none of the canvases by Mr. Robert Reid, in the dome of the Fine Arts

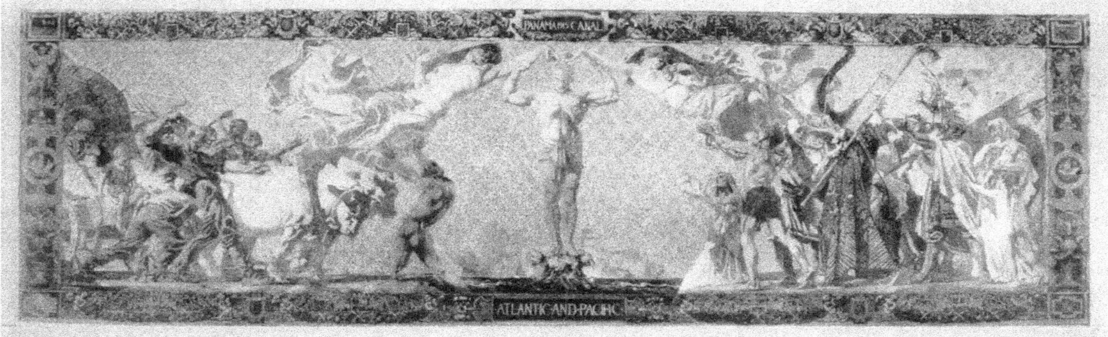

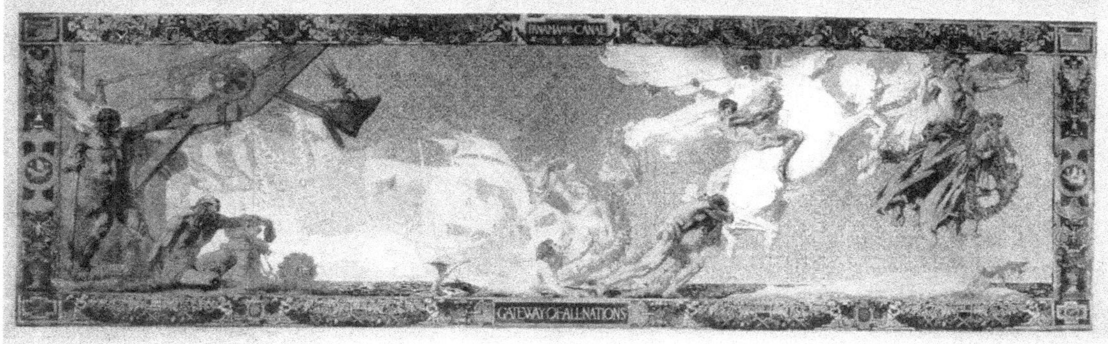

ATLANTIC AND
PACIFIC AND
THE GATEWAY
OF ALL NATIONS
WILLIAM
DE LEFTWICH DODGE,
PAINTER

Palace, can be said to do justice to the remarkable decorative talent of Mr. Reid. He is so well and prominently known as a painter of many successful decorations, in the East, that it is to be regretted that he was not in a happier mood when he came to the task of painting his eight panels of irregular shape for the Exposition.

The very scattered style of painting so effective in many of his easel paintings, which show all the fine qualities of a modern impressionistic school, is not of great help in pictures intended to be viewed from a great distance. His decorations present very little opportunity for the eye to rest upon them, and they are altogether too involved, in their turbulent compositions. Their color is not unattractive, no matter how cold, and of sufficient interest to atone for the lack of dignified design. The subjects of all of these are by no means unattractive, and a description of them reads far better than the pictures look.

The birth of European art is symbolized in the first panel. There are five dominant figures, grouped about an altar on which burns the sacred fire. An earthly messenger leans from his chariot to receive in his right hand from the guardian of the flame the torch of inspiration, while with his left hand he holds back his rearing steeds. In front of these a winged attendant checks for an instant their flight. The central figure, the guardian of the altar, still holds the torch, and below her are three satellites, one clasping a cruse of oil, another pouring oil upon the altar, while she holds in her hand a flaming brand, ready to renew the flame should it falter, a third zealously watching the fire as it burns. Opposite these a figure holds a crystal gazing-globe, in which the future has been revealed to her, but her head is turned to watch the flight of the earthly messenger.

The birth of Oriental art is symbolized in the second panel. The forces of the earth, wresting inspiration from the powers of the air, are pictured by a contest between a joyous figure in ancient Chinese armor, mounted upon a golden dragon, combating an eagle. A female figure under a huge umbrella represents Japan, while on either side are two other Oriental figures, in gorgeous attire, symbolic of the long periods of Oriental art.

The third panel represents the Ideals in Art. There are seven figures, the Greek ideal of beauty dominating all in a classic nude. Below this Religion is portrayed, in a Madonna and Child. Heroism is shown in Jeanne d'Arc, mounted on a war-horse and flinging abroad her victorious pennant. A young girl represents youth and material beauty, while at her side a flaunting peacock stands for absolute nature, without ideal or inspiration. A mystic figure in the background holds the cruse of oil. Over all of them floats a winged figure holding a laurel wreath for the victorious living, while a shadowy figure in the foreground holds a palm for the dead.

The fourth panel represents the inspirations of all Art, five figures symbolizing Music, Painting, Architecture, Poetry, and Sculpture. Flying above these are two winged figures, one holding a torch flaming with the sacred oil that has

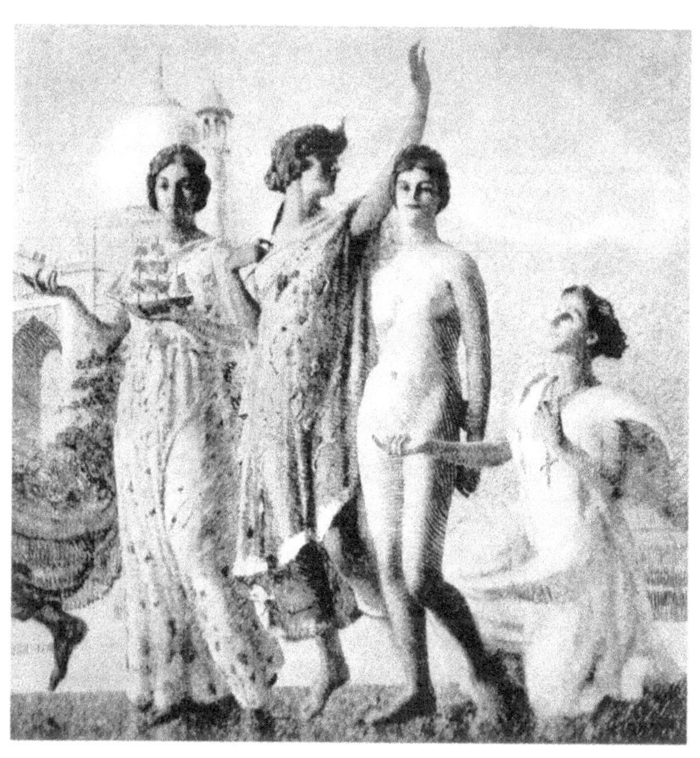

COMMERCE, INSPIRATION, TRUTH AND RELIGION
EDWARD SIMMONS, PAINTER

been brought from the altar, the other drawing back the veil of darkness, revealing the tangible, visible expression of Art to mortal eyes.

The four single panels symbolize the four golds of California; the poppies, the citrus fruits, the metallic gold, and the golden wheat. The idea of the four golds is particularly novel and will some day yield far more interesting results, and I hope the subject will not be allowed to lie idle. It is a very fine idea, too good not to be used permanently in some dignified building in California.

The Court of the Four Seasons offers a decorative scheme of eight panels above the doorways in the colonnades and two large panels in the orchestral niche on the south. All of these ten paintings were done by Milton Bancroft, one of the younger of the Eastern decorator-painters, who took his task seriously enough, without rising in any of his decorations above the conventional, with the exception of the "Autumn" and the two larger panels in the half dome.

All of the seven decorations belonging to the set of eight smaller ones are rather academic in their monotony of symmetrical compositions, not sufficiently relieved by variety of detail. These decorations have to excess what Reid's decorations are lacking in, namely, repose. Their coloring is quiet and in thorough harmony with the architecture.

Bancroft's two more importantly placed decorations are, fortunately, his best efforts. "Art Crowned by Time" and "Man Receiving Instruction in the Laws of Nature" are very effective in their stateliness and thoroughly decorative quality. They show the artist's allegiance to the great decorations of the Renaissance in many quaint ways of filling out the background spaces by puttos holding tablets, simple bits of architecture, and conventionalized trees. His figure of "Art" is unique among his figures in the decorative pattern used on the mantle which falls gracefully from her shoulders. All the other Bancroft decorations are devoid of this use of surface patterns, which are so helpful and interesting in decorative arrangement.

It is only a few steps from the Court of the Four Seasons into the Court of Palms. In entering through the orchestral niche one passes directly underneath the lunette which holds the very decorative canvas by Arthur Mathews, the acknowledged leader in the art of California. It must be said that it does not seem right, in the light of what has been contributed by men from elsewhere, that Mathews' superb talent should have been employed only in one panel. His "Victorious Spirit," a rich and noble composition, has certain enduring qualities which are not to be found in a single one of any of the others. Simply taken as a decoration, his picture is most effective by its richness of color, and without going into the question of its meaning, it is thoroughly satisfactory as a decoration.

Childe Hassam's lunette, said to represent "Fruit and Flowers," is almost anaemic alongside Mathews' fullness of expression. Nobody ever suspected Childe Hassam of being a decorator, no matter how admittedly important a place he holds in the field of easel painting. The composition of his decorations is frugal in

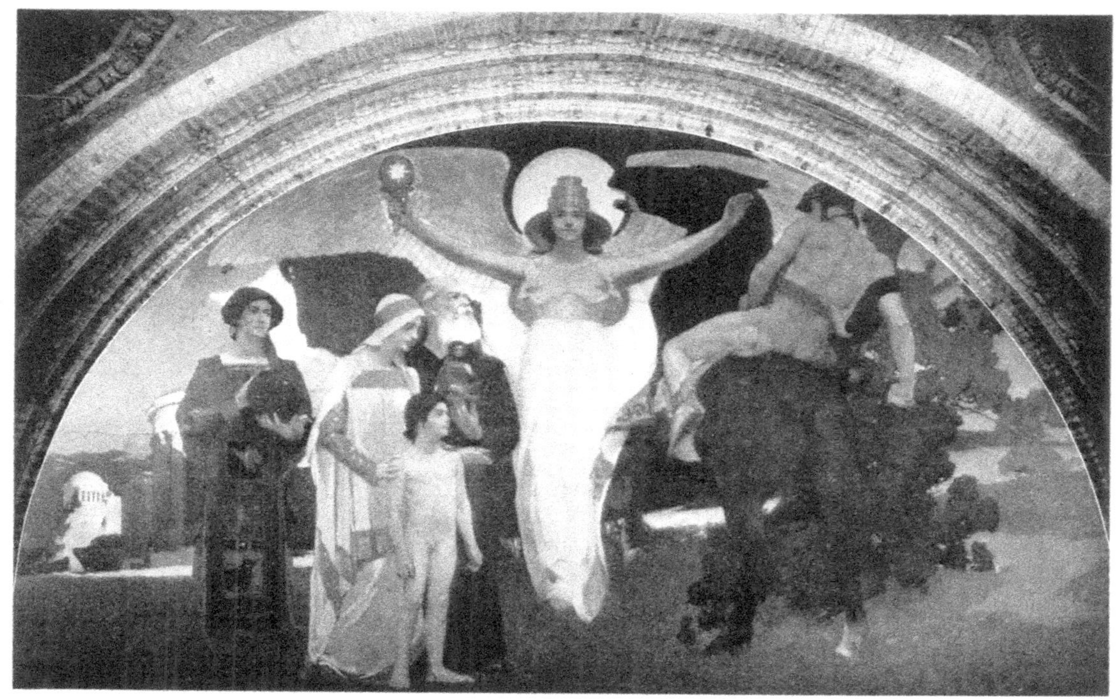

THE VICTORIOUS SPIRIT
ARTHUR F. MATHEWS, PAINTER

every sense, largely owing to the small scale of his figures. In the physical center of the composition nothing of interest happens, and the composition breaks almost in two. The coloring is insipid, and altogether not in keeping, in its extreme coldness, with the happy warmth of the travertine surrounding it.

Directly opposite, Charles Holloway presents himself in a very happy painting called "The Pursuit of Pleasure." A study of this picture can result in nothing but complete satisfaction. It is well and interestingly composed, lively in arrangement, in good scale, and not lacking in a certain feeling of repose, so essential in a good decoration, and, for that matter, in any work of art.

In the great arch of the Tower of Jewels the most elaborate decorations of Mr. William de Leftwich Dodge, of New York, command attention first of all by their fine and lively colors. These decorations show a most experienced artist, treating a wide variety of interrelated subjects with great skill. These enormous canvases, sixteen by ninety-six feet in size, are divided into a triptych, each picture continuing its central scheme into two smaller side panels.

The great composition to the left is labeled "The Atlantic and the Pacific," with a picture of "The Purchase" on the right and "The Discovery" on the left. Opposite we have the "Gateway of all Nations," with "Labor Crowned" and "The Achievement" on either side.

Mr. Dodge has a very fine sense of decoration, which he used with much skill. His command of human forms, together with the complete mastery of all other detail, enables him to paint very easily decorations which leave no doubt as to his long and varied experience in this field.

"The Atlantic and the Pacific" is very interesting in its formal symmetry, splendidly relieved by the individual treatment of the eastern and western nations which receive with expressions of joy the completion of the great waterway which means so much for the furthering of their mutual interests.

"The Gateway of all Nations" on the opposite side is less symmetrical, but very well balanced in its arrangement of many elements, naturalistic as well as allegorical. On the left, in the middle picture, one sees the retiring forces of labor, proudly watching the great procession of varied ships, moving in a joyous parade, led by Father Neptune and attendants, towards the recently opened gate. Preceding Father Neptune are allegorical figures, rhythmically swinging away into the sky. All of Dodge's decorations are good for their sound decorative treatment, always sustaining well the architectural surrounding frame, so particularly important in this great and massive tower. Dodge's backgrounds are devoid of any naturalistic suggestion, which so often destroys otherwise effective decorations.

The function of a decoration must always be to preserve the feeling of the wall, as opposed to the work of the easel painter, who wants to assist in forgetting that there is a canvas and to suggest that we are looking into the far

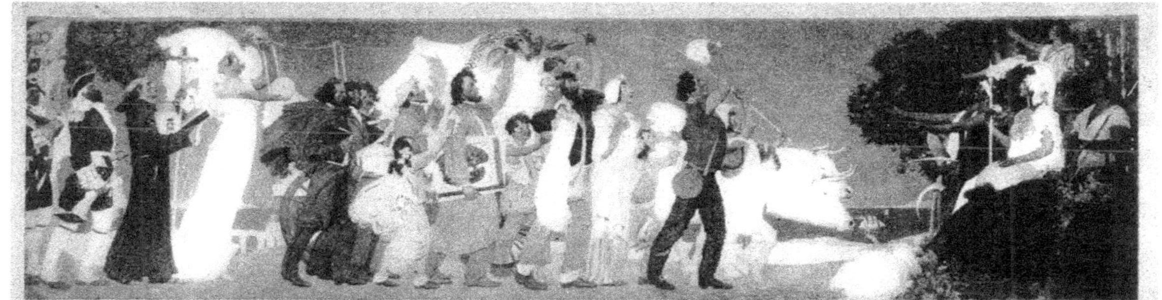

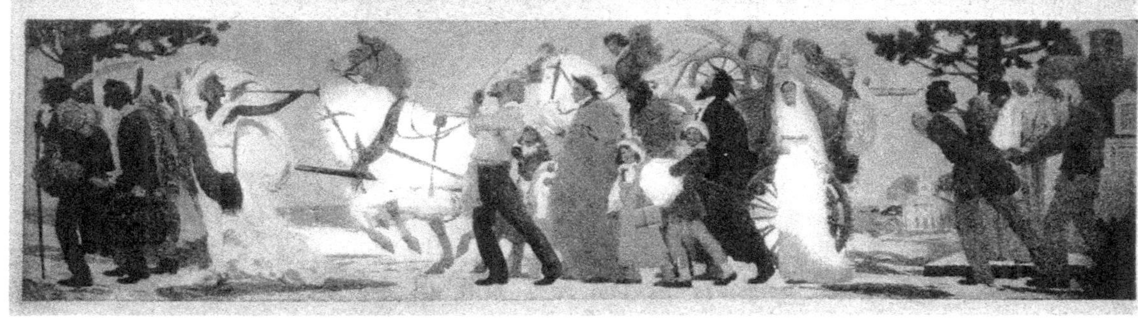

THE WESTWARD MARCH OF CIVILIZATION
FRANK V. DU MOND, PAINTER

distance. A good decoration should, as it were, allow the driving of a nail into any part of its surface—it should not make a hole in the wall.

In the two triumphal arches of the Nations of the East and the West, Frank Vincent Du Mond and Edward Simmons, respectively, contributed to the scheme of decorations. In the western arch, DuMond painted a continuous frieze of the march of civilization towards the great West. His work is most conscientiously done, very intellectual, and most effective in color, as well as in arrangement. You see in his continued scheme the entire story of western development.

It begins with the youth departing from his old father, who only reluctantly—feeling the infirmities of old age—stays behind. Preceding the young man, the historical prairie-schooner, accompanied by pioneers, continues the procession. This is developed further in historical groups of soldiers, priests, and men representing the intellectual rise of the great West. There is William Keith, with the palette, Bishop Taylor, Bret Harte, Captain Anza, and other well-known western figures, taking their place in the procession of tent wagons and allegorical figures, all striving towards that very fine group representing California in all the gorgeousness and splendor of the Golden State. This composition of "California," taken by itself, is one of the very best passages in the whole decoration, and could very effectively be used all by itself.

On the east, Edward Simmons presents two very charming compositions, full of great refinement and delicacy. The refined coloring of his decorations, so very delightful by themselves, is not in accord with the architecture, and in the overawing surroundings of the great arch they do not look as well as they might in a more intimate scheme of smaller scale. The one to the left, as seen from the Court of the Universe, tells of the dreams which led to the exploring and exploiting of the great West. Carefully designed figures of great refinement represent "Hope" and "Illusory Hope," scattering tempting bubbles, heading the procession of stately women. They are followed by "Adventure," "Art," "Imagination," "Truth," and "Religion" and a group suggesting family life.

On the opposite side the westward trend of War, Commerce, Conquest, Imagination, and Religion from all corners of the earth is typified.

Mr. Simmons in all his work employs a very unusual technique of broken columns, without losing a certain desirable simplicity of surface. His allegorical theme on the north side will linger in the minds of the people as one of the best of the Exposition decorations, particularly for its graceful drawing.

It seems hardly possible to do adequate justice to the very unusual genius of Frank Brangwyn, who charms thousands of Exposition visitors with his eight panels, representing the Four Elements, in the Court of Abundance. Brangwyn's pictures have one great advantage over all of the others, which lies in their accessible location, well controlled by daylight. All the other decorations seem to me to be situated too high above the ground. Brangwyn's have no such disadvantage to contend with. How

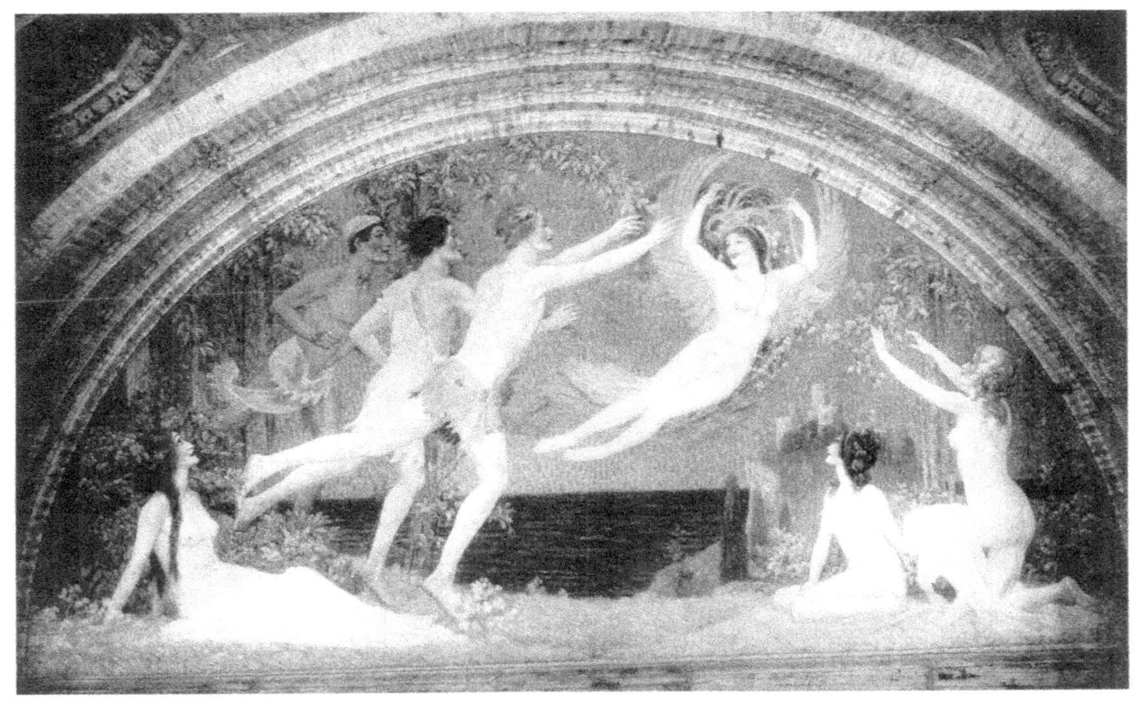

THE PURSUIT
OF PLEASURE
CHARLES HOLLOWAY
PAINTER

much more important, for instance, Mathews' lunette would look, placed somewhere nearer the level of the eye.

Brangwyn's canvases are a veritable riot of color, full of animation and life. They are almost dynamic. There seems to be something going on in all of them, all the time, and one hardly knows whether it is the composition, the color, or the subject, or all three, which gives them this very pronounced feeling of animation. He knows how to approach the extreme possibilities in pictorial decoration without losing sight of certain elements of repose. Seen from a distance, their effect at first is somewhat startling, owing to their new note, not reminiscent in the very least of the work of any other living—or past—painter. On closer examination they disclose a great wealth of form, very skillfully treated. There is every indication that it gave the artist the utmost pleasure to paint them. This spirit of personal enjoyment, which all of them convey in a remarkably sustained fashion, is contagious, and disarms all criticism. They are primarily great paintings in a technical sense. Added to that quality is a passionate love of pure color, juxtaposed with fine feeling for complementary colors of great intensity.

Brangwyn's glass window technique, of separation into many primary and secondary colors by many broad contrasts of neutral browns and grays, is very effective in bringing a feeling of harmony in all of his paintings, no matter how intense their individual color notes may be.

His pictures are not intellectual in the least, and all of the people in his pictures are animals, more or less, and merely interested in having a a square meal and being permitted to enjoy life in general, to the fullest extent.

The quality of enjoyment that runs through all of Brangwyn's work is extremely useful in the general atmosphere of Mullgardt's court. In the northwest corner, Nature is represented, in all the fecundity of the earth. Only in our wildest dreams, and only in the advertisements of California farm lands and orchards, do such grapes, pumpkins, pears, and apples exist.

The picture to the left shows the grape-treaders, in the old-fashioned and unhygienic practice of crushing grapes by dancing on them in enormous vats. Others are seen gathering and delivering more grapes. As in the other picture, showing the harvest of fruit, more people are shown. Brangwyn never hesitates to use great numbers of people, which seem to give him no trouble whatever in their modeling and characterization.

Following on to the right, "Fire," represented as the primitive fire and as industrial fire, in two pictures, continues the scheme. That group of squatting woodmen carefully nursing a little fire is almost comical, with their extended cheeks, and one can almost feel the effort of their lungs in the strained anatomy of their backs. There does not seem to be anything too difficult for Brangwyn. "Industrial Fire" is interesting from the decorative note of many pieces of pottery in the foreground. They seem to have come from the kiln which muscular men are attending.

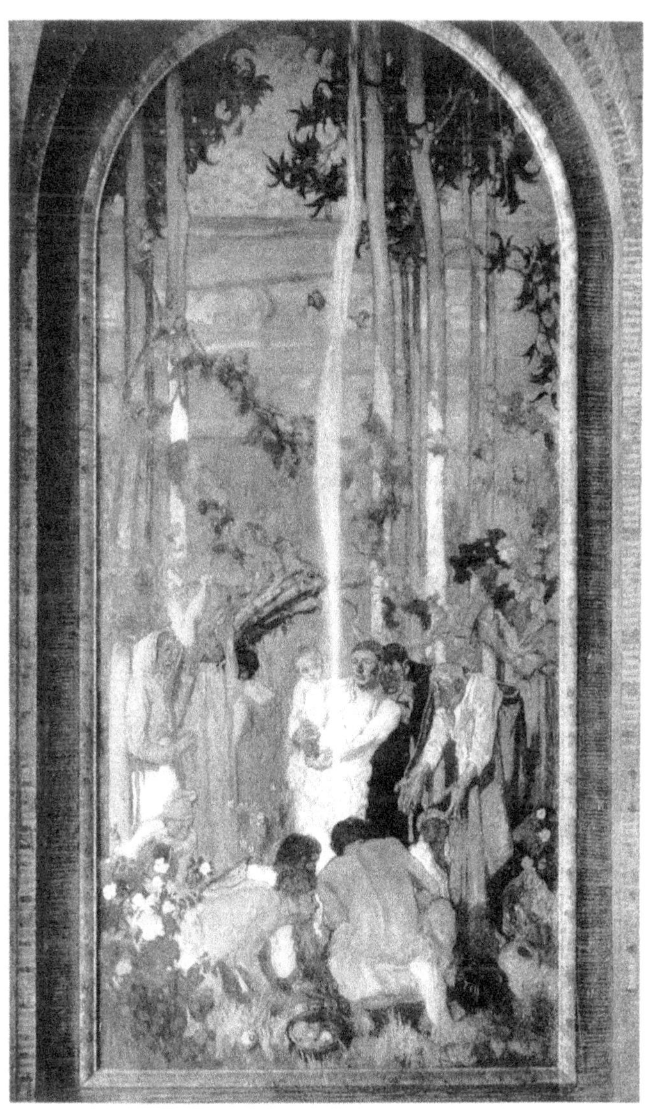

PRIMITIVE FIRE
FRANK BRANGWYN, PAINTER

"Water" is unusually graceful and delicate in its vertical arrangement of trees and the curve of the fountain stream, coming from the side of a hill. Women, children, and men have congregated, taking their turn in filling all sorts of vessels, some carried on their heads, some in their arms. Brangwyn's clever treatment of zoölogical and botanical detail is well shown in flowers in the foreground, such as foxglove and freesia, and the graceful forms of a pair of pinkish flamingoes. In the other panel of the same subject, a group of men on the shore are hauling in their nets.

The last of the four, "Air," represents this element in two totally different ways; the one on the left gives the more tender, gentle movement of this element, in the suggestion of the scent of the bowmen screened by trees, moving toward their prospective prey, while the other very bold composition is of a windmill turned away from the destructive power of an impending wind-storm. In the foreground people are rushed along by gusts of wind, while children, unaware of the impending storm, are flying kites.

The masterful and varied treatment of these eight canvases show Brangwyn as the great painter he is known to be. We should rejoice to have such excellent examples of his brush permanently with us.

While not exactly belonging to the number of official decorations, Edward Trumbull's wall-paintings in the unique Pennsylvania building are of great interest. Thoroughly dignified in their composition, they are most descriptive in their subject-matter. The "Pennsylvania Industries" are on the west side and "Penn's Treaty with the Indians" on the other. It is evident that Trumbull is a disciple of Brangwyn, though a personal note is not lacking in his work.

The tea-room of the California building harbors some mural decorations by Miss Florence Lundborg which the male part of the population can enjoy only by special invitation. I regret that they are not placed somewhere where the casual Exposition stroller can see them, because they are deserving of more attention than they are apt to receive. Miss Lundborg's artistic contributions have for many years been along the lines of decorations and in this big, well-composed figural scheme she discloses again a very fine, sympathetic understanding of the problems of a wall decoration. The color scheme is very refreshing and gives life to a large hall which has been endowed with unusual distinction by Miss Lundborg's art. A number of decorative floral medallions complete a scheme which is characterized throughout by dignity and sympathy.

THE ILLUMINATION
Conclusion

WHILE a daytime investigation of the Exposition no doubt has its rewards, the full meaning of the Exposition reveals itself at night. Never before has an Exposition been illuminated in the unique fashion of the Panama-Pacific International Exposition.

Former exposition lighting consisted of a lavish display of lighting fixtures, and of unavoidable millions of glaring bulbs, the number of which nobody was permitted to forget. The offensive glare of the direct light had to be eliminated to preserve that feeling of tonality, of restfulness, so impressive in daytime. In other words, the sources of all lights at night have been concealed, or so concentrated that they could be far removed, so as not directly to offend the eye. The effect is very much like the flood of light of a full-moon summer night.

In speaking of the rich mellowness of the lighting effect, one feels again compelled to speak of the travertine stucco as the artistic foundation of not only the architecture, sculpture, painting, and landscape garden effects, but also of the illuminating effects designed by Mr. W. D'A. Ryan, and executed by Mr. Guy L. Bayley. Without the mellow walls and rich orange sculptural details, no such picture of tonal beauty could have been produced.

It is difficult to single out, among the many suggestive pictures, the most alluring one, but I may safely say that the first half hour after the close of day, as enjoyed around the lagoon, with the Fine Arts Building in the background, reflected in the waters, will linger forever in the minds of all who are privileged to see it.

Such blues I have seen only in pictures by Maxfield Parrish. Combined with the rich gold of the colonnade, they are almost supernatural. The whole effect, as reflected in the placid surface of the lagoon, occasionally broken here and there by a slowly moving waterfowl, or the protruding mouth of a carp, is inspiring, and must awaken an aesthetic response in the soul of the most ordinary mortal. Very quickly, however, does this colorful picture change, and the very intense blue of the early evening sky rapidly changes into a colorless black.

The Palace of Fine Arts, above all others, offers many wonderful bits of enchantment at night. It seems to have been thought out not only for its daytime effect but for the night as well.

Of the inner courts, those with larger and smaller bodies of water are most effective at night. The Court of the Four Seasons, with its placid, shrub-encircled pool, is doubly interesting at night. The four wall-fountains add much to the outdoor feeling that this court possesses, by reason of the suggestive murmur of the waters, descending in gentle splashes from bowl to bowl.

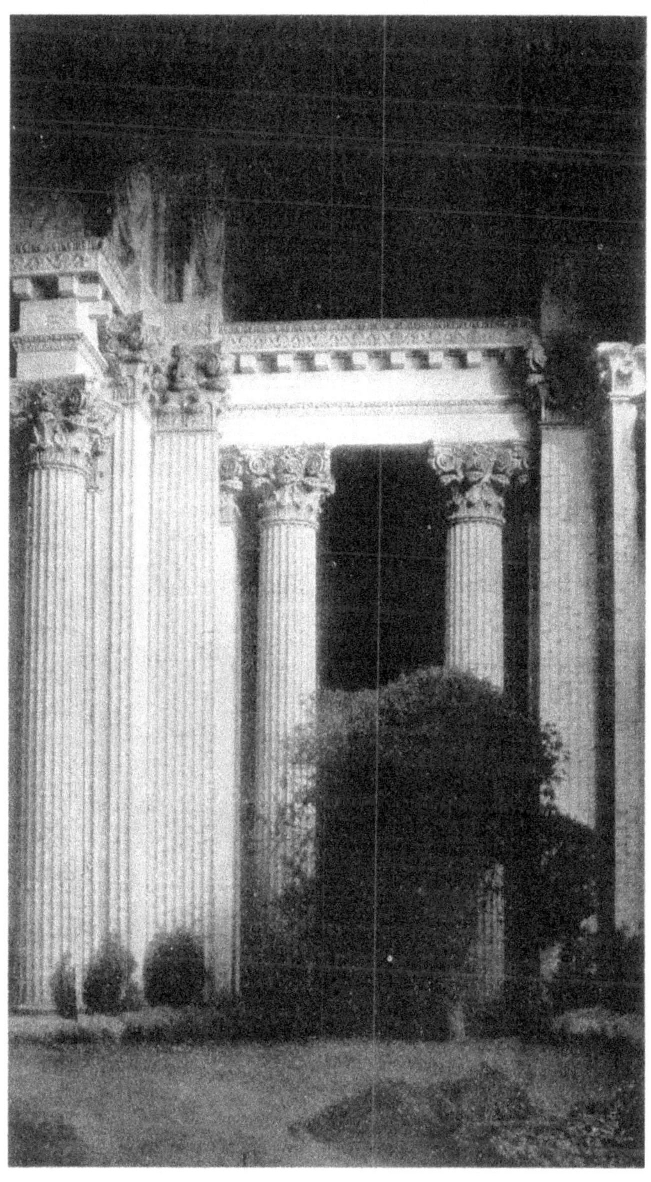

NIGHT EFFECT — COLONNADE OF THE PALACE OF FINE ARTS
BERNARD R. MAYBECK, ARCHITECT

The most striking court, in its mysteriousness, is Mullgardt's Court of Abundance, particularly so on a foggy night. Large volumes of vapor are lazily rising from huge bowls and torches, below, and in the tower, suggesting the early days of the cosmic All, cooling off from the turbulent period of its creation. The fogs sweeping from the bay add more mystery, and with the gorgeous perfume of the hyacinth carpet in the garden spaces, the effect is almost narcotic. The whole court, under these conditions, seems heavy with the atmosphere of abundance, of physical well-being, of slumbering natural powers.

At the same time, it is truly religious in its effect of turning the mind away from the ordinary world into the realm of the mystic and the supernatural. I never realized what our San Francisco fogs could produce in artistic effects until I visited Mullgardt's court on a foggy night. The effect of the fog is absolutely ennobling.

So many things like these, possibly not originally thought of, have added, together with the illumination, rare charm to the Exposition. Great masses of pigeons, attracted by the light thrown upon the two great groups of the Nations of the West and of the East, give an unusually inspiring touch to the Exposition at night. The spectacle of these graceful birds encircling rhythmically the great sculptural piles, apparently enjoying the bath of light, will never be forgotten. These pigeons seem to have decided to live in the Exposition; they are there always, and apparently glad to play their part in the Exposition ensemble.

The lesson of the Exposition will be far reaching in its many demonstrations of the commercial value of artistic assets. The whole Exposition is really a city-planning exposition of the first order. Any city-builder, by the respectful use of the great fundamental principles of balance, harmony, and unity, cannot help but do on a large scale what the Exposition presents in a more condensed fashion. I admit that we have made tremenduous strides in the remodeling of many of our large cities, particularly in the East, but we are still constantly starting new cities in the old planless way.

Our only practical and lasting effort in San Francisco along the lines of civic progress has been made in the civic center, where a far-reaching plan has been adopted and partly put into existence, and in some of our very charming newer restricted residence districts in the western end of the city, like St. Francis Wood, or in Northbrae and Claremont, in Berkeley, and elsewhere around the bay.

There is no doubt that we must better capitalize our own artistic assets, which we often allow to lie idle before we ever utilize them properly. The water front, Telegraph hill, the ocean shore, Sutro Heights, and Lincoln Park are all waiting to be developed in such a way as the Exposition suggests. The talk of cost is idle twaddle. If the Exposition, as an artistic investment, pays—and I see no reason whatever why it should not pay for itself—then we cannot do anything better than to invest our money wisely in other artistic improvements of a permanent character.

CONCLUSION

San Francisco is known all the world over for its unique location, rivaled only by that of Marseilles, and we have now the responsibility to use this natural asset, for which many envy us. The Exposition will start an avalanche of improvements along artistic lines which will be given increasing momentum by the development of long periods of prosperity.

The most urgent need, no doubt, is the establishment of a municipal art gallery in the civic center, the only ideal place for it, where the workingman from the Mission and the merchant from west of Van Ness avenue will find it equally convenient of access. If a smaller number of citizens could raise the money for a municipal opera house, there should be no trouble in getting funds for a building devoted to a far more extensive public benefit, like an art gallery. People generally will want to know why it is that certain things can be given to them for one year, so successfully, and why it should not be possible to have them with us permanently. The inspiring lesson of beauty, expressed so simply and intelligently, will sink deep into the minds of the great masses, to be reborn in an endless stream of aesthetic expression in the spiritual and physical improvement of the people.

We, out here in the West, have been measuring the tide of human progress in biological terms. We have almost forgotten the days of our great calamity, and still speak of them in that typical expression of apprehension of the "earthquake babies." Let us think now of the future and its bright prospects, inaugurated so auspiciously for the benefit of our Exposition generation.

APPENDIX

GUIDE TO SCULPTURE

SOUTH GARDENS:

Fountain of Energy (center) — *A. Stirling Calder*

Directly opposite the main entrance, the most conspicuously placed fountain in the grounds. The four major figures in the bowl represent the Pacific, the Atlantic, and the two Arctic oceans. The minor eight figures suggest the marine character of the fountain. The reclining figures on the sphere typify the two hemispheres. The youth on horseback represents energy and strength.

The Mermaid (fountains in long pools) — *Arthur Putnam*

The same figure is used twice, near the Horticultural Palace on the west and Festival Hall on the east.

Equestrian Statue, "Cortez" — *Charles Niehaus*

Guarding the Tower of Jewels. This statue represents the great Spanish conqueror. As one faces the tower, this figure is on the left.

Equestrian Statue of "Pizarro" — *Charles Cary Rumsey*

Similar in type and feeling to the preceding statue on the right, in front of the Tower of Jewels.

HORTICULTURAL BUILDING:

Frieze at Base of the Spires — *Eugene Louis Boutier*

Loose arrangement of standing female figures surrounding the bases of the spires on all sides of the Horticultural Palace, with no other meaning than that of decoration.

Pairs of Caryatides — *John Bateman*

Architectural vertical members supporting the pergola around the Horticultural Palace. Used also on the Young Women's Christian Association and the Press buildings, near the main entrance.

TOWER OF JEWELS:

Statues of "Priest," "Soldier," "Philosopher," and "Adventurer" — *John Flanagan*

Four figures suggestive of the forces which influenced the destinies of our country. Very big in scale—about twice life size. They are standing on a row of columns below the cornice on the tower and are repeated on all four sides.

The Armored Horseman (Terrace of the Tower) — *F. M. L. Tonetti*

A decorative equestrian statue on the lower terrace of the tower above the preceding figures—repeated sixteen times.

TOWER COLONNADES:

Fountain of Youth (east end) *Edith Woodman Burroughs*

Snugly placed inside the abutting walls, east of the Tower of Jewels. Naïve in character and simple in treatment, without any further symbolical meaning than that suggested by the name. Motif in side panels, "Ship of Life."

Fountain of El Dorado (west end) *Mrs. Harry Payne Whitney*

In position similar to the preceding, west of the Tower of Jewels. A triptych of dramatic expression, naturalistically treated.

FESTIVAL HALL:

Figure crowning the minor Domes *Sherry E. Fry*

A standing finial figure, on the minor domes, of graceful pose.

Two groups in front of the Pylons *Sherry E. Fry*

Practically conceived as wall fountains, they are composed of the figure of a girl, suggesting the joy of life, emphasized by young Pan, with a lizard, at the base on the left, and a seated young girl on the right.

Cartouche over the entrance (figures only) *Sherry E. Fry*

An architectural unit over the big arch of the main central dome, outside the building, for decorative effect.

Reclining figures on Pylons *Sherry E. Fry*

A male and a female figure, reclining, crowning the architectural units projecting into the South Gardens. Suggestive of life and pleasure.

COURT OF PALMS:

Equestrian statue, "The End of the Trail" *James Earl Fraser*

At the entrance of the Court of Palms, off the main avenue opposite the Horticultural Palace. Symbolical figure, representing the destinies of the vanishing red race; to be considered in connection with the "Pioneer" at the entrance of the Court of Flowers.

The Fairy (Italian Towers—Palms and Flowers) *Carl Grupp*

A figural termination of the four towers guarding the entrances to the Courts of Palms and of Flowers.

Caryatides *John Bateman and Mr. Calder*

Winged half-figure in the attic-space, repeated all around the court.

Spandrels *Albert Weinert*

Reclining decorative figures composed into the triangular spaces over all the doorways in the corridor.

COURT OF FLOWERS:

Equestrian statue, "The Pioneer" *Solon Borglum*

At the entrance of this court. Representing the white man and his victorious civilization. (To be studied with "The End of the Trail.")

SCULPTURE

Lions (at the entrances) — *Albert Laessle*

Very conventional architectural decorative animal forms at the entrance inside the Court of Flowers—used six times.

The Fairy (above the Italian Towers) — *Carl Gruppe*

[See Fairy under Court of Palms by the same artist.]

Central Fountain, "Beauty and the Beast" — *Edgar Walter*

Decorative fountain inside the court, with crowning figure of a young woman, reposing on a fabulous beast.

Flower Girls (in niches) — *A. Stirling Calder*

Repeated figures, conventionally treated, of young women, decorated profusely with flower garlands, in the attic space.

COURT OF ABUNDANCE:

Groups on the altar in the main tower — *Chester Beach*

These groups constitute the historical composition in the tower on the north side of the court. Beginning with the lower one, they represent the primitive ages, the middle ages, and modern times.

Group at column bases and finials — *Leo Lentelli*

Decorative figures. Used four times at the base of the shaft near the tower. A single finial figure of a girl with a bow is used on top of the same column.

Fountain of the Earth (central pool) — *Robert I. Aitken*

An architectural composition telling the story of human life in its many phases. The outstretched arms on the south side represent destiny giving and taking life.

Figures on top of the Arcade — *Albert Weinert*

Primitive men, with the pelican and deer; the mother with a child is repeated all around the court.

Aquatic Life (north extension) — *Sherry E. Fry*

A figure which might represent Neptune's daughter. This figure stands north of the tower in the open space toward the Marina below, between the Palaces of Transportation and Mines.

COURT OF THE UNIVERSE:

The Nations of the East; The Nations of the West

A. Stirling Calder, Leo Lentelli, and Frederick G. R. Roth, collaborators.

Colossal groups on top of the two great arches, representing, in many types, Western and Eastern civilization.

Statues on columns (eastern and western arches) — *Leo Lentelli*

Winged statues standing on top of columns on the inside as well as the outside of the two great arches.

Spandrels, Pegasus — *Frederick G. R. Roth*

Triangular compositions spanning the arches, repeated on both sides.

Medallion *B. Bufano*

Circular decorations of male figures on the left side of the arch without any meaning other than architectural effect.

Medallion *A. Stirling Calder*

Same as above, of female figures, on the right side of the arches.

The Stars (colonnades) *A. Stirling Calder*

Very conventional standing figure, with hands united above the head, forming a star with radiated head-dress, placed on the balustrades of buildings adjoining the court and in the avenue leading north from the court.

Frieze on corner pavilions, "Signs of the Zodiac" *Hermon A. MacNeil*

Decorative friezes on four sides of the four corner pavilions, of mythological character.

Two fountains, "The Rising Sun" and "The Setting Sun" *Adolph A. Weinman*

Two columns rising from fountain bowls and crowned by winged figures, of a woman, representing the Setting Sun, on the left, and of a winged male figure, the Rising Sun, on the right.

Four reclining figures, "The Elements" *Robert I. Aitken*

At the head of the stairs leading into the sunken garden; on the left, near the Music Pavilion, "Fire;" on the right, "Water;" on the left, near the tower, "Air;" on the right, "Earth."

Two Groups *Paul Manship*

Near the arches at the head of the steps, two figural groups. One is of female figures, suggesting pleasure; the other, music and art.

WESTERN PLAZA, IN FRONT OF MACHINERY PALACE:

Monument, "Genius of Creation" *Daniel Chester French*

Group of allegorical figures, suggestive of the development of the human race.

COURT OF THE FOUR SEASONS:

Four groups representing "The Seasons" *Furio Piccirilli*

In niches. Southeast corner, "Winter;" northeast corner, "Fall;" southwest corner, "Spring;" northwest corner, "Summer."

The Harvest (above the half dome) *Albert Jaegers*

Seated figure with a horn of plenty and other agricultural emblems.

Rain and Sunshine (figures on columns) *Albert Jaegers*

Standing female figures on columns on either side of the half dome. Sunshine, holding a palm branch, is on the left, and Rain, holding up a shell, on the right.

Groups, "Feast of Sacrifice," on the pylons in the forecourt. *Albert Jaegers*

SCULPTURE

The two groups on top of the building, in which huge bulls predominate, led by a young woman and a young man; very decorative.

Fountain, "Ceres" *Evelyn Beatrice Longman*

Situated half way between the Court of the Four Seasons and the Marina, in an avenue leading north; architectural in character.

Spandrels (arcade) *August Jaegers*

Reclining female figures above the arches at the west and east entrance of the Court of the Four Seasons.

Attic figures *August Jaegers*

Standing decorative figures of architectonic feeling, in the attic above the preceding figures.

VARIED INDUSTRIES PALACE:

Tympanum group in the doorway *Ralph Stackpole*

Groups of men and women in the lunette of the ornate doorway on the south side.

Secondary group, doorway *Ralph Stackpole*

Groups above the preceding one, showing Age transferring his burden to Youth.

Figure for niches, doorway (man with the pick) *Ralph Stackpole*

A repeated figure of a miner, of relatively small scale, on the consoles in the doorway.

Figure for keystone in doorway *Ralph Stackpole*

A small seated figure of a laborer, on the headstone.

Figure for niches, on the east façade of this Palace and of the Palace of Mines *Albert Weinert*

Standing figure in niches above doors, also used in avenue leading into the Court of Abundance from the east.

WEST WALL OF THE PALACES (facing Fine Arts):

Motifs for wall niches ("Triumph of the Field" and "Abundance") *Charles R. Harley*

Seated male and female figures surrounded by a great wealth of emblematic forms. The male represents "Triumph of the Field;" the female, "Abundance."

Figures on columns (flanking the half domes): Philosophy and Physical Vigor *Ralph Stackpole*

A colossal figure of a youth, on top of free-standing columns on the west wall of the main buildings.

PALACE OF FINE ARTS:

Standing figure, inside of the rotunda on top of columns *Herbert Adams*

Figures in the attic of the rotunda *Ulric H. Ellerhusen*

Standing females and males between architectural friezes immediately below the cupola of the dome.

Frieze on the altar *Bruno Louis Zimm*

Figural frieze at the base of the rotunda facing the Laguna can only be seen from a great distance across the water.

Relief panels for the rotunda *Bruno Louis Zimm*

Eight panels on the outside, of strictly architectural character, representing a procession, showing the development and influence of art.

Friezes around the base on the ground *Ulric H. Ellerhusen*

Figures with garlands, used everywhere at the base of the building.

Figures on the flower boxes *Ulric H. Ellerhusen*

Standing figures, looking inward, representing introspection.

Kneeling figure on the altar *Ralph Stackpole*

The shrine of worship. That delicate small figure seen best from across the laguna in front of the rotunda.

NORTH FAÇADE, MAIN GROUP OF EXHIBIT PALACES:

Figure for central niches, "Conquistador" *Allen Newman*

A Spanish soldier, with helmet and sword and a large mantle.

Figure for side niches, "The Pirate" *Allen Newman*

A coarsely shaped man, in small niches on the north side of the main buildings near the preceding one.

COLUMN OF PROGRESS:

Bas-relief (four sides of the pedestal) *Isidore Konti*

Four allegorical friezes depicting man's striving for achievement.

Finial group, "The Adventurous Bowman," frieze and decoration *Hermon A. MacNeil*

The group on top of the column suggests man's supreme effort in life, the supporting frieze is "The Toilers."

PALACE OF MACHINERY:

Figures on columns (four "Powers") *Haig Patigian*

Repeated large scale figures of men, representing the industries exhibited within the building.

Friezes for columns, vestibule *Haig Patigian*

Decorative architectural figure compositions of similar subjects.

Spandrels (two pairs) *Haig Patigian*

Reclining figures filling out the triangular spaces above the doors in the vestibule reflecting the purpose of the building.

PALACE OF EDUCATION:

Repeated figure within the Half Dome, of Thought *Albert Weinert*

Standing figure of a maiden with a scroll inside the portal, repeated eight times.

SCULPTURE

PALACE OF FOOD PRODUCTS:

Repeated figure within the Half Dome, "Physical Vigor" *Earl Cummings*

Similar to that above, inside the Portal of Vigor, showing a standing young man, with an oak wreath.

Friezes and figures in niches, main south entrance (portals of the Manufacturers and Liberal Arts Palaces) *Mahonri Young*

Figures representing domestic life and industries like foundry work, smithing, spinning, and sculpture. Figures in the niches: woman with spindles and men with hammers.

Tympanum panels (north and south entrances of the Palace of Education) *Gustave Gerlach*

Decorative panels above the doors outside of the building showing maternal instruction.

Panels inlaid in the walls over the minor entrances

Pupils of the School of Sculpture of the Society of Beaux Arts Architects and National Sculpture Society.

Decorative panels of school life and of science.

Figure, "Victory," on the gables of the palaces *Louis Ulrich*

A winged figure used on top of all the palaces.

MURAL DECORATIONS

COURT OF ABUNDANCE:

Earth *Frank Brangwyn*

Northwest corner of the corridor, two panels: grape-crushers on the left and fruit-pickers on the right.

Fire *Frank Brangwyn*

Two panels in the northeast corner of the corridor. Primitive Fire on the left and Industrial Fire on the right.

Water *Frank Brangwyn*

Two panels in the southeast corner of the corridor. Fountain motive on the left and fishermen hauling nets on the right.

Air *Frank Brangwyn*

Two panels in the southwest corner of the corridor. In the left panel, the scent of hunters carried toward their prospective prey. A windmill on the right.

COURT OF THE FOUR SEASONS:

Spring *H. Milton Bancroft*

Two murals above the doorway in the colonnade (southwest corner). To the left, Spring; to the right, Seedtime.

Summer *H. Milton Bancroft*

Two murals similar to those in the northwest corner of the court. Fruition on the right; Summer on the left.

Autumn *H. Milton Bancroft*

In the northeast corner of the court, two panels: Autumn on the right; Harvest on the left.

Winter *H. Milton Bancroft*

Similar in location to the preceding, in southeast corner. Two murals, Festivity on the right; Winter on the left.

Man Receiving Instruction in Nature's Laws *H. Milton Bancroft*

One upright panel, in the half dome on the right.

Art Crowned by Time *H. Milton Bancroft*

On the left opposite the preceding.

EASTERN ARCH, COURT OF THE UNIVERSE:

Hope and Attendants: (On the north wall) *Edward Simmons*

THE MURAL DECORATIONS

Historical types: (On the south wall) *Edward Simmons*

Representing Greece, Italy, Spain, England and France, on the south wall.

TOWER OF JEWELS:

The Atlantic and Pacific (in the center); The Discovery (on the left;) The Purchase (on the right) *William de Leftwich Dodge*

Gateway of All Nations (in the center); Labor Crowned (on the left); Achievement (on the right) *William de Leftwich Dodge*

Six panels inspired by the construction of the Panama Canal. The first group is on the west wall, the second on the east.

WESTERN ARCH, COURT OF THE UNIVERSE:

The Westward March of Civilization, in two panels by *Frank V. DuMond*

Beginning in the north panel and continued in the opposite one.

COURT OF PALMS:

Fruits and Flowers *Childe Hassam*

Painting in a lunette over the entrance into the Palace of Education.

The Pursuit of Pleasure *Charles Holloway*

A painting of the same shape as the preceding, over the entrance into the Palace of Liberal Arts.

The Victorious Spirit *Arthur Mathews*

In the lunette over the doorway into the Court of the Four Seasons.

ROTUNDA, PALACE OF THE FINE ARTS:

The Four Golds of California (Golden Metal, Wheat, Citrus Fruits, and Poppies) *Robert Reid*

In the ceiling inside the rotunda.

Art, born of flame, expresses its ideals to the world through music, poetry, architecture, painting, and sculpture *Robert Reid*

In the same location.

Birth of European Art. Birth of Oriental Art *Robert Reid*

Belonging to the preceding group of eight pictures by the same artist.

PENNSYLVANIA BUILDING:

Decorative Paintings *Edward Trumbull*

In the east and west walls of the center court of the building, showing Penn's Treaty with the Indians on the right and Pennsylvania Industries on the left.

BIOGRAPHICAL NOTES

ADAMS, HERBERT	(Sculptor) New York. Born in West Concord, Vermont, 1858. Studied in Paris. Figures on columns inside of Rotunda, Palace of Fine Arts.
AITKEN, ROBERT I.	(Sculptor) New York. Born in San Francisco, California, 1878. Studied in Mark Hopkins Institute, San Francisco, and Paris. The Four Elements, in Court of the Universe, and Fountain of Earth in Court of Abundance.
BACON, HENRY	(Architect) New York. Born in Watseka, Illinois, 1866. Studied at the University of Illinois and in Europe. Court of the Four Seasons
BAKEWELL AND BROWN	(Architects). John Bakewell, Jr., San Francisco. Born in Topeka, Kansas, 1872. Studied at the Beaux Arts, Paris. Arthur Brown, Jr. San Francisco. Born in Oakland, California, 1874. Studied in the University of California and at the Beaux Arts in Paris. Horticultural Palace.
BATEMAN, JOHN	(Sculptor) New York. Born in Cedarville, New Jersey, 1877. Studied in the School of Industrial Arts, Philadelphia, and in Paris. Caryatides outside of Horticultural Building.
BAYLEY, GUY L.	(Electrical Engineer) San Francisco. Born in Vacaville, California, 1875. Studied at University of California. Chief of Electric and Mechanical Department.
BEACH, CHESTER	(Sculptor) New York. Born in San Francisco, California, 1881. Studied in Paris, New York and Rome. Groups on tower on Court of Abundance.
BENNETT, EDWARD	(Architect) Chicago. Preliminary Plans of Exposition.
BITTER, KARL	(Sculptor). Born in Vienna, Austria, 1867. Died April 10, 1915, New York. Studied at Vienna Academy of Fine Arts. Chief of Sculpture.
BLISS AND FAVILLE	(Architects) Walter D. Bliss, San Francisco. Born in Nevada, 1868. Studied in the Massachusetts Institute of Technology and abroad. William B. Faville, San Francisco. Born 1866. Studied in the Massachusetts Institute of Technology. Main Buildings forming center unit of eight Palaces.
BOBERG, FERDINAND	(Architect) Stockholm. Born in Falun, Sweden, 1860. Swedish Building.
BORGLUM, SOLON H.	(Sculptor) New York. Born in Ogden, Utah, 1868. Studied in Art Academy of Cincinnati and in Paris. The Pioneer.

BOURGEOIS, JEAN LOUIS (Architect). Born in Autun, France, 1876. Died February 26, 1915, in France. Collaborated with Bakewell and Brown in Horticultural Building design.

BOUTIER, EUGENE LOUIS (Sculptor). Frieze at Base of Spires on Horticultural Building.

BRANGWYN, FRANK (Painter) London. Born in Bruges, Belgium, 1867. Mural paintings of the Four Elements in the Court of Abundance.

BUFANO, B. (Sculptor) New York. Medallions on the arches in Court of the Universe.

BURDITT, THOMAS H. (Architect) San Francisco. Born in Nellore, India, 1886. California State Building.

BURROUGHS, MRS. EDITH WOODMAN (Sculptor) Flushing, Long Island. Born in Riverdale-on-Hudson, 1871. Studied in Art Students League of New York and in Paris. Fountain of Youth.

CALDER, A. STIRLING (Sculptor) New York. Born in Philadelphia, 1870. Studied in Pennsylvania Academy of Fine Arts and in Paris. Acting Chief of Sculpture. Fountain of Energy; The Star in Court of the Universe; Flower Girl in Court of Flowers; Nations of the East, Nations of the West, in collaboration with F. Roth and Leo Lentelli.

CARRERE AND HASTINGS (Architects) John M. Carrere, deceased. Thomas Hastings, New York. Born New York, 1860. Studied in Beaux Arts, Paris. Tower of Jewels.

CUMMINGS, M. EARL (Sculptor) San Francisco. Born in Salt Lake City, Utah, 1876. Studied in San Francisco and Paris. Repeated figure in Portal of Vigor, Palace of Food Products.

DENNEVILLE, PAUL E. (Architectural Sculptor) New York. Born in Ancy, France, 1873. Studied Cooper Institute New York, and abroad. Travertine finish of buildings.

DODGE, WILLIAM DE LEFTWICH (Mural Painter) New York. Born in Liberty, Virginia, 1867. Studied in Munich and Paris. Two Murals in Tower of Jewels.

DUMOND, FRANK V (Painter) New York. Born in Rochester, New York, 1865. Studied in Paris. Two Murals in arch of Setting Sun.

ELLERHUSEN, ULRIC H. (Sculptor) New York. Figures in attic of Rotunda and repeated friezes at base of Fine Arts Building.

FARQUHAR, ROBERT DAVID (Architect) Los Angeles. Born in Brookline, Massachusetts, 1872. Studied at Harvard and at Beaux Arts, Paris. Festival Hall.

FLANAGAN, JOHN (Sculptor) New York. Born in Newark, New Jersey, 1865. Studied in Boston, New York and Paris. Figures on Tower of Jewels.

FRASER, JAMES EARL (Sculptor) New York. Born in Winona, Minnesota, 1876. Studied in Paris. The End of the Trail.

FRENCH, DANIEL CHESTER (Sculptor) New York. Born in Exeter, New Hampshire, 1850. Studied in Boston, New York and Florence. Genius of Creation.

FRY, SHERRY E. (Sculptor) New York. Born in Creston, Iowa, 1879. Studied in Art Institute, Chicago, and in Paris. Figural decorations on Festival Hall.

GARNETT, PORTER (Writer) Berkeley. Born in San Francisco, California, 1871. Selection of inscriptions on monuments and arches.

GERLACH, GUSTAVE (Sculptor) Weehawken, New Jersey. Tympanum panels north and south entrances Palace of Education.

GRUPPE, CARL (Sculptor) New York. Fairy figure on Italian towers.

GUERIN, JULES (Painter) New York. Born in St. Louis, Missouri, 1866. Studied in America and abroad. Director of color and decoration. Color scheme.

HARLEY, CHARLES R. (Sculptor) New York. Born in Philadelphia, Pennsylvania, 1864. Studied in Pennsylvania Academy of Fine Arts and in Paris. "The Triumph of the Field" and "Abundance," on west facade of main buildings.

HASSAM, CHILDE (Painter) New York. Born in Boston, Massachusetts, 1859. Studied in Paris. Lunette, Fruits and Flowers, in Court of Palms.

HOLLOWAY, CHARLES (Painter). Lunette, The Pursuit of Pleasure, in Court of Palms.

HORNBOSTEL, HENRY (Architect) New York. Born in Brooklyn, New York, 1867. Studied in New York and Paris. Pennsylvania State Building.

HOWARD, JOHN GALEN (Architect) Berkeley. Born in Chelmsford Massachusetts, 1864. Studied in Boston and Beaux Arts, Paris. Exposition Auditorium in the Civic Center in collaboration with Frederick Meyer and John Reid, Jr.

JAEGERS, ALBERT (Sculptor) New York. Born in Elberfeld, Germany, 1867. Studied abroad. Figures of Harvest, Rain and Sunshine, and Bulls in Court of Four Seasons.

JAEGERS, AUGUST (Sculptor) New York. Born in Barmen, Germany, 1878. Studied in Paris. Spandrels and attic figures in Court of Four Seasons.

KELHAM, GEORGE W. (Architect) San Francisco. Born in Manchester, Massachusetts, 1871. Studied at Harvard. Director of Architecture. Courts of Palms and Flowers.

KONTI, ISIDORE (Sculptor) New York. Born in Vienna, Austria, 1862. Studied in Imperial Academy, Vienna. Frieze at base of Column of Progress.

LAESSLE, ALBERT (Sculptor) Philadelphia. Born in Philadelphia, Pennsylvania, 1877. Studied in Philadelphia. Lions in Court of Flowers.

LENTELLI, LEO — (Sculptor) New York. Born in Bologna, Italy, 1879. Figures on decorative shafts in Court of Abundance; Nations of the East and Nations of the West in collaboration with Stirling Calder and Frederick Roth.

LONGMAN, MISS EVELYN BEATRICE — (Sculptor) New York. Born in Winchester, Ohio, 1874. Studied in Chicago and New York. Fountain of Ceres.

LUNDBORG, FLORENCE — (Painter) San Francisco. Born in San Francisco. Studied in San Francisco and in Paris. Mural decorations in Tea Room of the California Building.

McKIM, MEAD AND WHITE — (Architects) New York. Living members of the firm: William R. Mead. Born in Battleboro, Vermont, 1846. Studied at Amherst and in Europe. W. Symmes Richardson. W. Mitchell Kendall. Court of the Universe.

McLAREN, JOHN — (Landscape Engineer) San Francisco. Born in Scotland. Horticultural effects.

MACNEIL, HERMON A. — (Sculptor) New York. Born in Everett, Massachusetts, 1866. Studied in Boston and Paris. Adventurous Bowman and frieze of Toilers on Column of Progress.

MANSHIP, PAUL — (Sculptor) New York. Groups in Court of Universe.

MARKWART, ARTHUR — (Engineer) San Francisco. Born in Illinois, 1880. Studied at University of California. Assistant Chief of Construction. Structural design of Machinery Palace.

MATHEWS, ARTHUR F. — (Painter) San Francisco. Born in Wisconsin, 1860. Studied in Paris. Lunette, the Victorious Spirit, in Court of Palms.

MAYBECK, BERNARD R. — Architect) San Francisco. Born in New York, 1862. Studied in Beaux Arts, Paris. Palace of Fine Arts.

MEYER, FREDERICK — (Architect) San Francisco. Born in San Francisco, California, 1875. Studied in America. Exposition Auditorium in Civic Center in collaboration with John Galen Howard and John Reid, Jr.

MULLGARDT, LOUIS CHRISTIAN — (Architect) San Francisco. Born in Washington, Missouri, 1866. Studied at Harvard. Court of the Ages, also named Court of Abundance.

NAHL, PERHAM W. — (Painter) Berkeley. Born in San Francisco, California, 1869. Studied in Hopkins Institute, San Francisco, and in Europe. Exposition Poster, "The Thirteenth Labor of Hercules."

NEWMAN, ALLEN G. — (Sculptor) New York. Born in New York, 1875. Pupil of J. Q. A. Ward. Conquistador and Pirate on north facade main buildings.

NIEHAUS, CHARLES H. — (Sculptor) New Rochelle, New York. Born in Cincinnati, Ohio, 1855. Studied in Cincinnati and Munich. Cortez.

PATIGIAN, HAIG — (Sculptor) San Francisco. Born in Armenia, 1876. Studied in Paris. Decorations of Machinery Hall.

PICCIRILLI, FURIO (Sculptor) New York. Born in Massa, Italy, 1866. Pupil of Accademia San Luca, Rome. Groups of Four Seasons in Court of the Four Seasons.

POLK, WILLIS (Architect) San Francisco. Preliminary plans of Exposition.

PUTNAM, ARTHUR (Sculptor) San Francisco. Born in New Orleans, 1874. Mermaid in South Gardens.

REID, JOHN, JR. (Architect) San Francisco. Born in San Francisco, 1880. Studied in the University of California and the Beaux Arts, Paris. Exposition Auditorium in Civic Center in collaboration with John Galen Howard and Frederick Meyer.

REID, ROBERT (Painter) New York. Born in Stockbridge, Massachusetts, 1862. Studied in Boston, New York, and Paris. Decorations in Rotunda of Fine Arts Palace.

ROSSE, HERMANN (Designer and decorator) Palo Alto. Born in The Hague, Holland, 1887. Studied at The Hague, at Delft, Holland, and South Kensington, London. Decorative color scheme and mural painting in Netherlands Building.

ROTH, FREDERICK G. R. (Sculptor) Englewood, New Jersey. Born in Brooklyn, New York, 1872. Studied in Vienna. Nations of the East and Nations of the West in collaboration with Stirling Calder and Leo Lentelli.

RUMSEY, CHARLES CARY (Sculptor) New York. Pizarro.

RYAN, WALTER D'ARCY (Electrical Engineer) San Francisco. Born in Kentville, Nova Scotia, 1870. Educated in Canada. Chief of Illumination. Lighting scheme.

SIMMONS, EDWARD (Mural Painter) New York. Born in Concord, Massachusetts, 1852. Studied in Paris Murals in Arch of the Rising Sun.

STACKPOLE, RALPH W. (Sculptor) San Francisco. Born in Oregon, 1885. Studied in Paris. Kneeling figure in front of Fine Arts rotunda. Figures on columns flanking Portal of Thought and Portal of Vigor. Figures in doorway of Palace of Varied Industries.

TONETTI, F. M. L. (Sculptor) New York. Born in Paris, France, in 1863. Studied in Paris. Armored horseman on Tower of Jewels.

TRUMBULL, EDWARD (Painter) Pittsburgh. Born in Stonington, Connecticut, in 1884. Mural decorations, Penn's Treaty and Pittsburgh Industries, in Pennsylvania Building.

ULRICH, LOUIS (Sculptor) New York. Winged Victory on gables of all palaces.

WALTER, EDGAR (Sculptor) San Francisco. Born in San Francisco, in 1877. Studied in Paris. Fountain of Beauty and the Beast in Court of Flowers.

Weinert, Albert	(Sculptor) New York. Born in Leipzig, Germany, in 1863. Studied in Leipzig and Brussels. Spandrels in Court of Palms; Decorative finial figure, in Court of Abundance repeated figure in Portal of Thought, etc.
Weinman, Adolph A.	(Sculptor) New York. Born in Karlsruhe, Germany, in 1870. Studied in Art Students League, New York. Rising and Setting Sun.
Ward and Blohme	(Architects) Clarence R. Ward, San Francisco. Born in Niles, Michigan, in 1870. Studied in America. J. H. Blohme, San Francisco. Born in San Francisco in 1878. Studied in America. Machinery Palace.
Whitney, Mrs. Harry Payne	(Sculptor) New York. Fountain of El Dorado
Young, Mahonri	(Sculptor) New York. Born in Salt Lake City, Utah, in 1877. Studied in New York and Paris. Frieze over main portals Manufacturers and Liberal Arts Palaces.
Zimm, Bruno Louis	(Sculptor) New York. Frieze, Rotunda, Fine Arts Building.

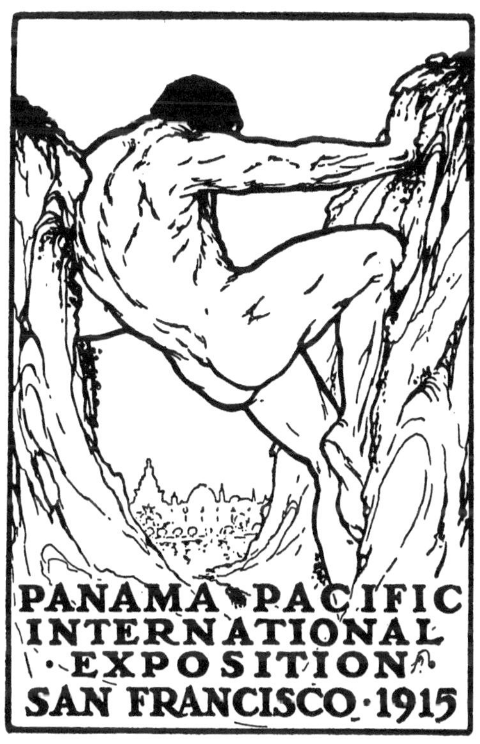

OFFICIAL POSTER
PERHAM W. NAHL

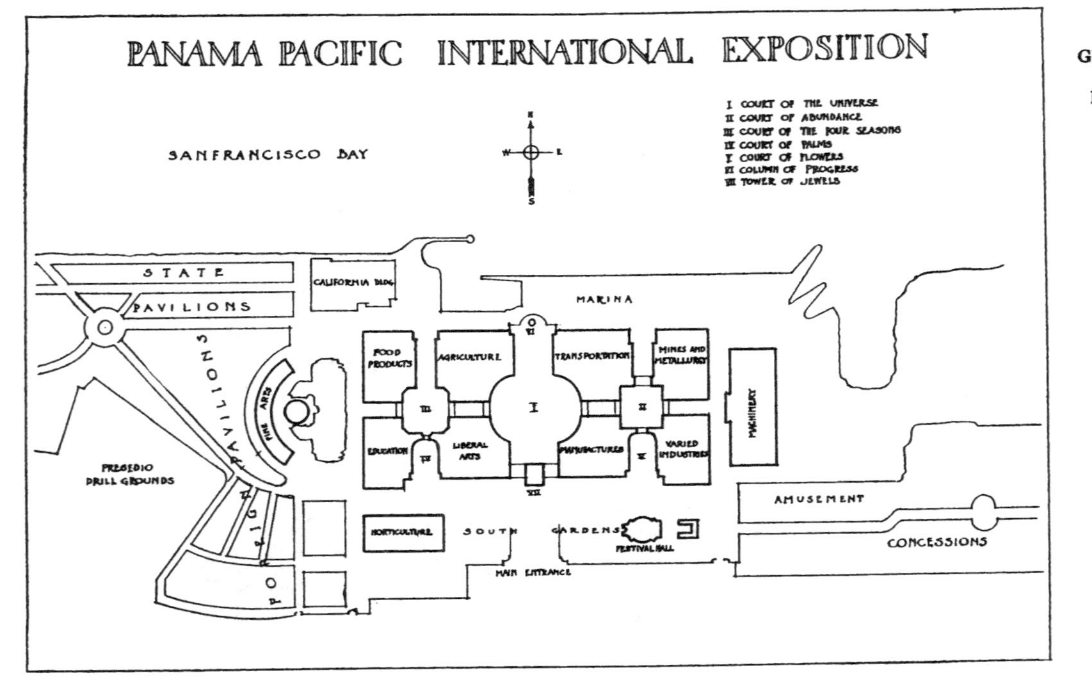

GROUND PLAN OF THE EXPOSITION

THE ART OF THE EXPOSITION, BY EUGEN NEUHAUS, PUBLISHED BY PAUL ELDER AND COMPANY, SAN FRANCISCO, WAS PRINTED AT THEIR TOMOYE PRESS, UNDER THE DIRECTION OF JOHN SWART, IN MAY AND REPRINTED IN JUNE AND AGAIN IN AUGUST NINETEEN HUNDRED AND FIFTEEN

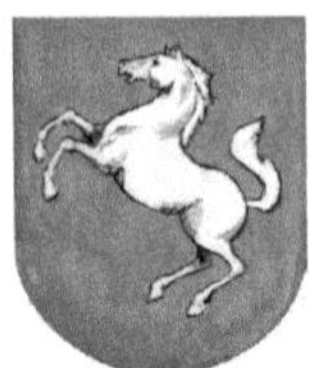

Featured Titles from Westphalia Press

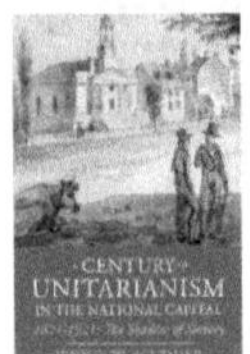

A Century of Unitarianism in the National Capital, 1821-1921 by Jennie W. Scudder

Jennie Scudder's work traces the sometimes controversial history of Unitarianism in the District of Columbia, centering on All Souls Unitarian Church. The account includes the development in the District and surrounding towns in northern Virginia and Southern Maryland.

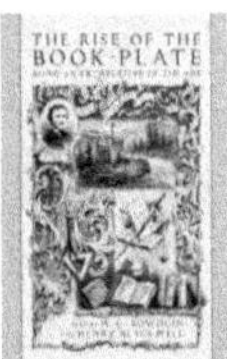

The Rise of the Book Plate: An Exemplative of the Art by W. G. Bowdoin, Introduction by Henry Blackwel

Bookplates were made to denote ownership and hopefully steer the volume back to the rightful shelf if borrowed. They often contained highly stylized writing, drawings, coat of arms, badges or other images of interest to the owner.

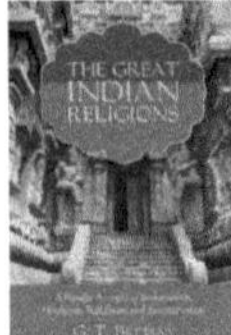

The Great Indian Religions by G. T. Bettany

G. T. (George Thomas) Bettany (1850-1891) was born and educated in England, attending Gonville and Caius College in Cambridge University, studying medicine and the natural sciences. This book is his account of Brahmanism, Hinduism, Buddhism, and Zoroastrianism

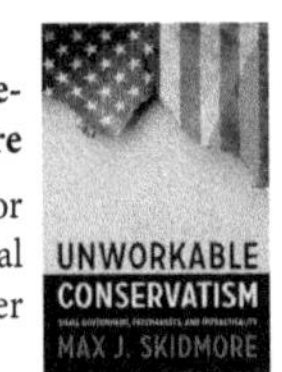

Unworkable Conservatism: Small Government, Freemarkets, and Impracticality by Max J. Skidmore

Unworkable Conservatism looks at what passes these days for "conservative" principles—small government, low taxes, minimal regulation—and demonstrates that they are not feasible under modern conditions.

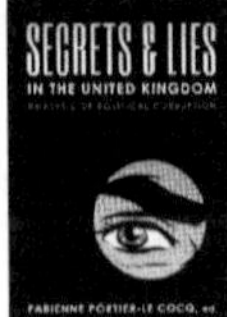

Secrets & Lies in the United Kingdom: Analysis of Political Corruption
Edited by by Fabienne Portier-Le Cocq

Secrets & Lies in the United Kingdom: Analysis of Political Corruption lifts the shroud of secrecy in the United Kingdom in relation to modern freemasonry in Scotland in the late-18th century, the 'Stolen Generations' in Australia from the early 1900s to the late 1970s, and so much more.

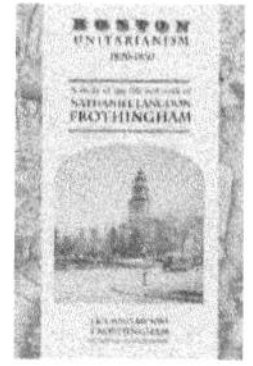

Boston Unitarianism 1820-1850
by Octavius Brooks Frothingham

From the author, "Many years ago I proposed writing something in memory of Dr. Frothingham, but abandoned the project on account of the meagerness of the biographical material. Within the twelvemonth, a warm friend and admirer of his asked me to prepare a memoir."

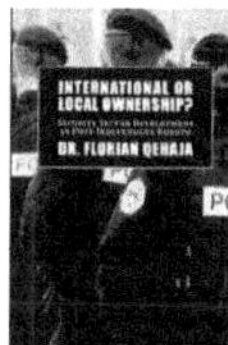

International or Local Ownership?: Security Sector Development in Post-Independent Kosovo
by Dr. Florian Qehaja

International or Local Ownership? contributes to the debate on the concept of local ownership in post-conflict settings, and discussions on international relations, peacebuilding, security and development studies.

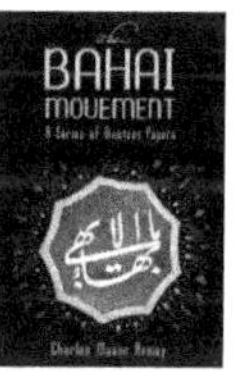

The Bahai Movement: A Series of Nineteen Papers
by Charles Mason Remey

Charles Mason Remey (1874-1974) was the son of Admiral George Collier Remey and grew up in Washington DC. He studied to be an architect at Cornell (1893-1896) and the Ecole des Beaux Arts in Paris (1896-1903), where he learned about the Baha'i faith, and quickly adopted it.

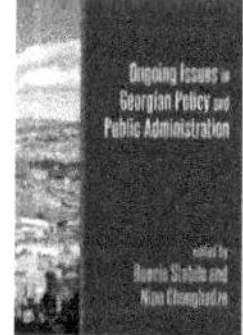

Ongoing Issues in Georgian Policy and Public Administration
Edited by Bonnie Stabile and Nino Ghonghadze

Thriving democracy and representative government depend upon a well functioning civil service, rich civic life and economic success. Georgia has been considered a top performer among countries in South Eastern Europe seeking to establish themselves in the post-Soviet era.

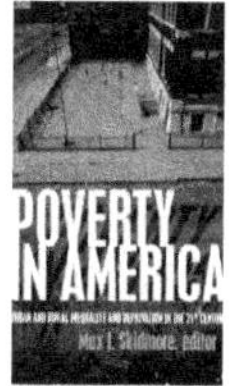

Poverty in America: Urban and Rural Inequality and Deprivation in the 21st Century
Edited by Max J. Skidmore

Poverty in America too often goes unnoticed, and disregarded. This perhaps results from America's general level of prosperity along with a fairly widespread notion that conditions inevitably are better in the USA than elsewhere. Political rhetoric frequently enforces such an erroneous notion.

www.ingramcontent.com/pod-product-compliance
Lightning Source LLC
LaVergne TN
LVHW010618100826
845148LV00014B/3027